KEEPING THE SABBATH WHOLLY

KEEPING
THE SABBATH
WHOLLY

Ceasing, Resting, Embracing, Feasting

Marva J. Dawn

WILLIAM B. EERDMANS PUBLISHING COMPANY
GRAND RAPIDS, MICHIGAN

We gratefully acknowledge permission to quote material from the following publications:

Excerpts from *My Mother's Sabbath Days* by Chaim Grade. Copyright © 1986 by the Estate of Chaim Grade. Reprinted by permission of Alfred A. Knopf, Inc.

Excerpts from *The Sabbath* by Abraham Joshua Heschel. Copyright
© 1951 by Abraham Joshua Heschel. Copyright © renewed 1979
by Sylvia Heschel. Reprinted by permission of Farrar, Straus &
Giroux, Inc.

DEDICATION

This book is dedicated to all the people who need the Sabbath—

*the busiest, who need to work from a cohesive,
unfragmented self;*

social activists, who need a cycle of worship and action;

*those who chase after fulfillment and need to understand
their deepest yearnings and to hear the silence;*

*those who have lost their ability to play because of the
materialism and technologization of our society, who need
beauty and gaiety and delight;*

*those who have lost their passion and need to get in touch
with feelings;*

those who are alone and need emotional nourishment;

those who live in community and need solitude;

*those who cannot find their life's priorities and
need a new perspective;*

*those who think the future is dictated by the present, who
need hope and visions of the future to
change the present order;*

*those who long for deeper family life and want to
nurture certain values;*

*the poor and the oppressed, who need to mourn and to
dance in the prison camp;*

*the rich and the oppressors, who need to learn nonviolence,
stewardship, and God's purposes in the world;*

*those who suffer, who need to learn how
suffering can be redemptive;*

*professional theologians, who need to bring the
heart back into theology;*

*those who don't know how religion fits into the modern
world, who need a relationship with God;*

*those who are disgusted with dry, empty, formalistic
worship and want to love and adore God;*

*those who want to be God's instruments, enabled and
empowered by the Spirit to be
world changers and Sabbath healers.*

Contents

Preface   x

I: CEASING   1

1. Ceasing Work   5

2. Ceasing Productivity and Accomplishment   17

3. Ceasing Anxiety, Worry, and Tension   22

4. Ceasing Our Trying to Be God   28

5. Ceasing Our Possessiveness   36

6. Ceasing Our Enculturation   41

7. Ceasing the Humdrum and Meaninglessness   48

Contents

II: RESTING   **51**

8. Spiritual Rest   55

9. Physical Rest   65

10. Emotional Rest   72

11. Intellectual Rest   78

12. Aids to Rest   84

13. Social Rest   88

14. An Ethics of Character   95

III: EMBRACING   **99**

15. Embracing Intentionality   103

16. Embracing the Values
of the Christian Community   111

17. Embracing Time instead of Space   119

18. Embracing Giving instead of Requiring   124

19. Embracing Our Calling in Life   131

20. Embracing Wholeness—*Shalom*   137

21. Embracing the World   145

IV: FEASTING   **149**

22. Feasting on the Eternal   153

23. Feasting with Music   166

Contents

24. Feasting with Beauty   173

25. Feasting with Food   180

26. Feasting with Affection   189

27. Feasting and Festival   195

28. Sabbath Ceasing, Resting, Embracing, and Feasting   203

Appendix: A Few Suggestions for Rituals to Begin and End the Sabbath Day   212

Works Cited   215

Preface

B UT, MOMMY, I don't wanna go to church!"
How often I have heard that plaintive cry—and not
only from the young! What a sad commentary it is on
North American spirituality that the delight of "keeping the Sabbath day" has degenerated into the routine and drudgery—even
the downright oppressiveness—of "going to church."

This phrase is both negative and limiting. In the first place,
how we talk affects how we live. To say "I am going to church"
both reveals and promotes bad theology. In the earliest days of
Christianity, "the church" was a living and vibrant gathering of
God's *people,* who met together to be strengthened and then went
out into the world to manifest the gospel in their actions and
their very beings. Now the church has become a static *place,* to
which believers go for tired and tiring rituals. We are NOT "going
to church"! We are going to a *sanctuary* to participate in an *order
of worship* together with other *people of God* gathered in *community,* to be nourished by all that we do there together so that we
can go out into the world and *be church.*

In the second place, the act of worship is only one small
part (though an essential one) of the whole meaning of Sabbath

keeping. To "keep the Sabbath holy" means to recognize that the rhythm of six days of work and one day of ceasing work is written into the very core of our beings. To observe that order week by week creates in us a wholeness that is possible only when we live in accordance with this pattern of being graciously commanded by God.

I will not enter into the debate about whether the Sabbath should be observed on Saturday, the true seventh day of Jewish custom, or on Sunday, set apart by the earliest Christians as the Lord's Day.[1] There are many reasons for emphasizing either choice. It has worked best for my own understanding of my faith to observe a Sabbath day (thus thankfully appreciating the roots of my faith in the insights, practices, and disciplines of the Hebrew people and responding to the commandment to keep the Sabbath holy), but to practice my Sabbath customs on Sunday (to recognize the Resurrection as the decisive event for Christian faith and life). Most of the suggestions in this book can be applicable to either Saturday or Sunday celebrations. The important thing is that a particular day is set aside as the Sabbath, and that it is observed faithfully every seven days so that God can imbue us with his rhythm of six days of work and one day of ceasing work.

This book will sketch many of the results of Sabbath keeping—the effects of our ceasing, resting, embracing, and feasting. The observance of such an ordering of our days preserves more wholistically the fabric of our existence. Truly, the wholeness of being the people of God is desperately needed in our lopsided and fragmented age and ardently desired by those who profess that faith in God makes a difference in one's lifestyle.

Many of the points of this book are related to one's daily disciplines of devotional life, because many of the things that I

---

1. An excellent overview of the issues is presented by Willard M. Swartley's *Slavery, Sabbath, War, and Women: Case Issues in Biblical Interpretation* (Scottdale, Penn.: Herald Press, 1983), especially pp. 65-95. This is an excellent book for learning how to use the Scriptures in dealing with ethical questions.

write about are the results of our consistent practices for growing in our relationship with God. However, contemporary Christians and Jews need to remember and celebrate again that God
himself deliberately established the rhythm of six days of work
and one day of ceasing work in order that this relationship could
reach greater depth.

It disturbs me that so many of the books and articles describ-
ing the disciplines of the spiritual life contain no mention whatsoever of observing the Sabbath. We find exhortations to practice
celebration, chastity, confession and absolution, fasting, fellowship,
frugality, meditation, mutuality, prayer, service, silence, simplicity,
solitude, study, submission, tithing, and worship. All of these are
valuable, and most of them are related to Sabbath keeping.
However, the particular discipline of remembering the Sabbath is
specifically inculcated in the ten covenant commandments of
Yahweh.

In *The Table of Inwardness,* Calvin Miller stresses that intimacy with God cannot be rushed, that we cannot enjoy the presence of God if we are always looking at our watches.[2] That is
why keeping the Sabbath is so important—because on that day
we never wear our watches at all. Except for attending certain
specific hours of worship and Bible class, we have the whole day
long to move as the Spirit leads us.

Many of you are probably saying by now, "But that's impossible! I can't get through an entire day without wearing my
watch. I have too much to do." That is the very reason you need
this book. I can *promise* you that if you develop a lifestyle in which
you spend one day as a Sabbath day without wearing a watch,
you will be more able to accomplish all that you have to do on
the days that you wear one.

To keep the Sabbath is not a legalistic duty. Rather, living
in accordance with our own natural rhythm gives freedom, the
delight of one whole day in every seven set apart as holy. Come

---

2. Miller, *The Table of Inwardness* (Downers Grove, Ill.: InterVarsity
Press, 1984), pp. 35-36.

with me into the experience of observing the Sabbath, and you will discover for yourself—or rather, *in* yourself—the meaning of holy time.

Please don't be frustrated if you are unable to integrate all of the ideas of this book into your own lifestyle. Sabbath keeping is never meant to be legalistic. (As Jesus said, "The Sabbath was made for humankind, not persons for the Sabbath"—Mark 2:27, my translation.) Do what you gladly choose to do. Each of us is able to utilize different disciplines depending upon our circumstances and commitments. I have many freedoms as a single person, not tied to the usual sort of job, that give me opportunities not available to others. I do not want you to adopt blindly any of the ideas included in this book. My goal is to make clear how practical the notion of keeping the Sabbath is and how many benefits are attendant upon such practice.

The Sabbath is accessible to everyone and involves many different kinds of pathways. I am reminded of many Impressionist paintings of landscapes dominated by roads, rivers, paths, and railroads to emphasize the accessibility of the countryside and to invite us to imagine ourselves in its beauty. I pray that the ideas in this book will invite you into your own unique paths for observing and enjoying the Sabbath.

This book is filled with ideal descriptions of what it could be like if we were able perfectly to celebrate the Sabbath day and keep it holy. Ideals are useful if we hold them up before us as visions; we can never reach those ideals in this life, but they show us the direction in which we choose to walk. I hope and pray that this book will stir in you the desire to put into your life more Sabbath customs, more Sabbath freedom, more Sabbath delight, a Sabbath spirituality.

Also, please do not infer from my descriptions that I am good at keeping the Sabbath. The process of writing this book has reinforced my desire to practice keeping the Sabbath more carefully, because I am not at all close to practicing these visions as faithfully as I would like. I have a lot to learn about celebrating the Sabbath, and I am very grateful to all the people, especially the Jewish teachers, who have taught me whatever I know about Sabbath delight. I apologize to contemporary Jews for any mistakes I may have made in understanding your customs; I hope you will inform me of my failures to appreciate your Sabbath traditions correctly. I am grateful for the many lessons Christians can learn from our roots in Judaica for our own worship of God through the practice of Sabbath keeping.

I owe a great debt of gratitude to my former editor, Roy M. Carlisle, who was instrumental in developing the basic structure of this book according to the themes of ceasing, resting, embracing, and feasting. I also wish to thank especially all the people who have given me ideas for this book—particularly those people attending retreats or workshops at which I have spoken about Sabbath keeping. Please accept my gratitude, although I cannot list all the names I carried home with me on countless scraps of paper.

Dorothy Day, the founder (with Peter Maurin) of the Catholic Worker movement, writes about a great German Protestant theologian who said after the Second World War that what the world needed was community and liturgy.[3] Those are two of the major components of Sabbath keeping, and certainly they are very much needed today. The immense popularity of Richard Foster's *Celebration of Discipline*,[4] published in 1978, makes us realize that there is a deep hunger for spiritual growth in our society, although Foster did not focus on the discipline of Sabbath keeping. However, in 1982 Tilden Edwards emphasized the concept of "Sabbath time"[5] for the Christian world, and in 1987 Karen Burton Mains stressed the importance of "making Sunday special."[6]

---

3. Cited in Day, *The Long Loneliness: An Autobiography* (San Francisco: Harper & Row, 1981), p. 222.

4. Foster, *The Celebration of Discipline: Paths to Spiritual Growth* (San Francisco: Harper & Row, 1978).

5. Edwards, *Sabbath Time: Understanding and Practice for Contemporary Christians* (New York: Seabury Press, 1982).

6. Mains, *Making Sunday Special* (Waco, Tex.: Word Books, 1987).

This book attempts to go beyond these previous works by bringing together Hebrew practices and Scripture, our contemporary Christian understanding of who we are as the people of God, and a deeper comprehension of the meaning of ceasing, resting, embracing, and feasting. Accordingly, this book combines these things: theologizing about various aspects of our Christian beliefs related to Sabbath keeping; stories that illustrate various dimensions of ceasing, resting, embracing, and feasting; descriptions of particular customs that I have developed as a Christian observing the Sabbath; references to biblical passages that relate to the issues; and a necessary bit of combatting some heresies that threaten our contemporary understanding of what it means to be Christians seeking spiritual discipline without legalism.

This book is designed with four sections of seven chapters each. Each section could be used for a week of quiet-time devotions. The shorter chapter for the seventh day would allow more time on Saturday for preparations for the next day's Sabbath celebration. Another possibility would be to read one section on four consecutive Sabbath days so that its ideas could be thought about in the coming week in preparation for the next Sabbath keeping. However you choose to read the book, I pray that you will put its contents into actual practice and not only into your head as good ideas. This is not a book about the Sabbath; it is a plea for Sabbath keeping.

In Judaica the Sabbath is loved as a bride or a queen. Deep in our beings there is a longing for completion, and all sorts of prostitutes in our culture compete to satisfy that yearning. Only holy time, in which we experience the presence of God, can fill our emptiness. When we focus on our love for the bride, nothing else matters. May our growing together to understand the meaning of Sabbath keeping give you the opportunity to fall in love with the Sabbath Queen and thereby love more deeply the King of the Universe!

*Blessed art Thou, O Lord our God, King of the universe,
who hast sanctified us by Thy commandments, and
commanded us to kindle the Sabbath lights.*

*May the Sabbath-light which illumines our dwelling
cause peace and happiness to shine in our home. Bless
us, O God, on this holy Sabbath, and cause Thy divine
glory to shine upon us. Enlighten our darkness and guide
us and all mankind, Thy children, towards truth and
eternal light. Amen.*

—opening prayer of the
traditional home service for Sabbath eve

PART I
CEASING

*And God blessed the Sabbath day and made it holy,
because on it he ceased from all the work of creating that
he had done.*

—Genesis 2:3

*Come, let us welcome the Sabbath in joy and peace! Like a
bride, radiant and joyous, comes the Sabbath. It brings
blessings to our hearts; workday thoughts and cares are
put aside. The brightness of the Sabbath light shines forth
to tell that the divine spirit of love abides within our home.
In that light all our blessings are enriched, all our griefs
and trials are softened.*

—from the Kiddush ritual of a
Reform home service for Sabbath eve

WE START WITH the importance of ceasing on a day set apart as holy because the name *Sabbath* comes originally from the Hebrew verb *shabbat*, which means primarily "to cease or desist." In Exodus 31:16-17 we are told that "the Israelites are to observe the Sabbath, celebrating it for the generations to come as a lasting covenant" because it is "a sign between me [the LORD]¹ and the Israelites forever, for in six days the LORD made the heavens and the earth, and on the seventh day he abstained from work and rested." Hebrew scholars translate the last phrase as "he ceased and was refreshed." Genesis 2:2 literally says that God "ceased" on the seventh day.

We will consider many aspects of Sabbath ceasing— to cease not only from work itself, but also from the need to accomplish and be productive, from the worry and tension that accompany our modern criterion of efficiency, from our efforts to be in control of our lives as if we were God, from our possessiveness and our enculturation, and, finally, from the humdrum and meaninglessness that result when life is pursued without the Lord at the center of it all. In all these dimensions we will recognize the great healing that can take place in our lives when we get into the rhythm of setting aside every seventh day all of our efforts to pro-

---

1. All the letters of LORD are capitalized in our English versions to translate the Hebrew word *Yahweh* (sometimes rendered "Jehovah"). Since the Jews never enunciated this word in order not to blaspheme God's name, we can only guess at its pronunciation. This is the name, usually translated "I AM," by which God introduced himself to Moses at the burning bush when Moses asked who was sending him to the Israelites and to Pharaoh (Exod. 3:13-15). This name is used 6,823 times in the Hebrew Scriptures (compared with 2,570 uses of the title *Elohim*). The name emphasizes the covenant faithfulness of the God of Israel, who intervenes in history to save his people. In frequently using the phrase "I AM" in the Gospel of John (see, for example, John 13:19 and 8:58), Jesus claims for himself the divinity of the covenant God, the LORD of the Hebrew people.

vide for ourselves and make our way in the world. A great benefit of Sabbath keeping is that we learn to let God take care of us—not by becoming passive and lazy, but in the freedom of giving up our feeble attempts to be God in our own lives.

1. Ceasing Work

MOST AMERICANS WORK five days a week and then spend the weekend trying to do everything that needs to be done around the house and yard. Consequently, the Sabbath day (whether that be observed on Saturday or Sunday) is not a day of ceasing from work because the pressure of the work that "needs to be done" at home matches the pressure of the work that earns one's salary. To cease working on the Sabbath means to quit laboring at anything that is work. Activity that is enjoyable and freeing and not undertaken for the purpose of accomplishment (see the next chapter) qualifies as acceptable for Sabbath time.

To advocate a complete day of ceasing from work—as this entire book does—does not mean, of course, that work is wrong. Indeed, our work is worship when we do it to the glory of God. However, that subject must be pursued at another time, for our focus here is on the rhythm of the worshipful life, alternating between regular days of work and a special day of ceasing, resting, embracing, and feasting.

To cease working is the original meaning of Sabbath underscored by the expansion of God's instructions concerning the

Israelite feasts in Leviticus 23. The Sabbath command is proclaimed as follows:

> There are six days when you may work, but the seventh
> day is a Sabbath of rest [literally, a ceasing], a day of sacred
> assembly. You are not to do any work; wherever you live,
> it is a Sabbath to the LORD (v. 3).

First of all, we must note that the day is "a Sabbath to the
LORD"; in other words, it is a ceasing in order to honor the
covenant God. Sacred assemblies were held for the same reason—to gather the children of Israel together to worship Yahweh. Moreover, the Sabbath is a day of ceasing work, no matter
where one lives (which might emphasize that even farmers are
included). The people of God were commanded not to do any
work, no matter what their social location.

We might wonder, then, about doctors and nurses, pastors
and musicians, and other service practitioners who have to work
on Sundays. On the one hand, we must avoid any sort of legalism
about Sabbath keeping. Jesus himself healed on the Sabbath, and
yet the Gospels strongly and frequently affirm that he faithfully
observed the Sabbath. Preaching a sermon, playing an instrument
for worship or in the symphony, or ministering to the sick might
not be "work" for some of us. We dare not be legalistic about
what constitutes work.

On the other hand, some people will necessarily have to make
their Sabbath another day besides Saturday or Sunday if it is to be
a day without work. If such "re-scheduling" is necessary, the important thing is to make that day of ceasing from work a consistent
habit,[1] a regular rhythm of keeping the Sabbath every seven days.
I have seen several articles urging pastors to make a weekday their

---

1. It grieves me that our society usually thinks of the word *habit*
only in the sense of bad habits. I will be using the word very positively in this book to stress the value of developing spiritual disciplines,
which keep us more aware of the objective presence of God, especially during the times when we are not able subjectively to feel good about

Sabbath day,[2] and for several years I observed the Sabbath on Tuesday. We dare not be legalistic about which day is considered one's seventh day—hence I'm not too bothered by the argument about whether the Sabbath must be Saturday or Sunday. We lose the freedom of the gospel if we become too legalistic about that issue. What God wants from us is a whole day that we set apart to honor him by gathering with a sacred assembly and by ceasing from work—a day that is a Sabbath ceasing unto Yahweh. Perhaps those people, such as nurses and pastors, who must labor on Sundays could form small groups to set aside another day to assemble for worship and to cease working for the entire day.

The key to experiencing the Sabbath in the richness of its design is to recognize the importance of its rhythm. Which day is used to observe the Sabbath is not as important as ensuring that the day of ceasing occurs every seven days without fail. Throughout this book we will see the benefits of such an orderly rhythm, but we will notice especially the freedom that such a discipline creates. As Calvin Miller reminds us, "Learn to obey. Only he who obeys a rhythm superior to his own is free."[3]

God's design of the Sabbath rhythm was never meant to impose a legalistic duty. As the Old Testament scholar Brevard Childs emphasizes in his commentary on Exodus, the close juxtaposition of the passage on the laws given on Sinai with the passage on the covenant relationship of God and his people "guards against a legalistic interpretation of the law apart from the covenant, on the one hand, and, on the other hand, against an alleged covenant of grace conceived of without a content." We New Tes-

---

our relationship with God. Consistent habits of reading one's Bible, spending time in prayer, meditating on God's Word, participating in fellowship opportunities with other Christians, and observing the Sabbath day with various customs all serve as channels for God's grace to flow into and through our lives even when we can't feel it.

2. See, for example, Eugene H. Peterson's "Confessions of a Former Sabbath Breaker," *Christianity Today*, 2 Sept. 1988, pp. 25-28.

3. Miller quoting Nikos Kazantzakis in *The Table of Inwardness* (Downers Grove, Ill.: InterVarsity Press, 1984), p. 78.

tament people need the biblical witness of the Hebrew Scriptures
to correct our false spiritualizing of the covenant and the demands
of its law.[4] We need to learn again the psalmists' delight in the
law as God's instruction for true blessing in our lives. (See, for
example, Psalms 1, 19, and 119.)

To recognize the delight of the Sabbath covenant instruction, we might each remember a time when we were under
tremendous pressure to finish a certain project, some job that
demanded the utmost of our energy and resources, some work
that caused us to long for the day when we would be finished.
What a relief when at last we completed the task and our efforts
could cease! No doubt we laughed with delight and had a party
to celebrate the end of our slaving.

I remember the old days when I had to type all my book
manuscripts on a typewriter. The last version was a terrible drag
to complete because I had already been over the material half
a dozen times, and now it was necessary to type it one last time.
(Oh, how grateful I am to be writing for the first time on a word
processor!) Whenever I had finally finished the last page of the
last chapter, I would call up my secretary, who would immediately come over with her husband and a half gallon of ice cream.
It was such a huge relief to be done at last that we had to celebrate!

Now imagine what a glorious relief it can be *every week* to
know that in the rhythm of our lives there is one day in every
seven on which we can cease our working. That knowledge gives
us all kinds of energy to keep at tasks for the other six days, since
we know that soon it will be time to rest. Furthermore, ceasing
from work for one day enables us to return to it with renewed
vigor as the new week begins. Thus, that day of ceasing empowers
us both as we anticipate and as we remember its benefits. (See
Section II of this book.)

I learned the tremendous freedom of ceasing work a few

---

4. Childs, *The Book of Exodus: A Critical, Theological Commentary*
(Philadelphia: Westminster Press, 1974), pp. 382-84.

years ago during the summer-school session at the University of Notre Dame. I had already been trying to keep the Sabbath faithfully for a year, but my practice was tested in a new way when, with the requirement of proficiency in five languages for my Ph.D. program, I had to take French, German, and Latin all at once.

The only way for me to keep the three languages straight was to devise an arduous study schedule beginning each morning at six. (I'm not a morning person, so that was a terrible chore from the start.) I worked on Latin till class at nine, after which I studied German till that class. French study and class took half the afternoon, and then I'd swim awhile to stay in shape (and cool my brain!). Returning home, I continued working on French till dinner, and then studied German till I went to bed at eleven. Each night I dropped into bed utterly exhausted, but the intense pace was necessary since, after only six weeks of class, I had to be able to translate a thousand words in a two-hour test in each language.

What enabled me to keep following this absurd schedule every day was my anticipation, celebration, and remembrance of the Sabbath. Toward the end of the week, the knowledge that Sabbath would soon come gave me incredibly powerful comfort and courage to persist, even as, at the beginning of the week, memories of the Sabbath delight I had just experienced motivated me to begin again. And on Sundays ceasing to work at languages set me free for lots of fun.

Every Sunday I enjoyed worship and Bible study, ate different foods than I ate during the rest of the week, and engaged in relaxing and creative activities. Sometimes I played the organ for worship, went to the beach or swimming pool, took long walks, or played in the parks in the afternoon with friends or by myself. Most of all, Sunday was a day for enjoying God's presence.

Rarely have I experienced such *vast* relief in the Sunday ceasing from work as I did that summer, but each week I do experience a lovely moment of release when at last I go to bed on Saturday night. I tell you the truth: I sleep differently on Saturday nights because the Sabbath has begun.

That sweet moment of relief is directly related to a particular

Jewish custom that helps us begin our Sabbath keeping more effectively. Again, I must emphasize that I don't want any of my suggestions to be legalistic—to imply that you *must* do a certain thing in order to observe the Sabbath properly.

Most modern societies conceive of the day as beginning first thing in the morning. By contrast, Jews begin the Sabbath at sundown on Friday in keeping with their notion of the day—that it lasts from sunset till sunset. Since I prefer the Jewish concept, but have not managed to be ready by sunset, my Sabbath observance begins when I lie down to sleep on Saturday night. That way my sleep is a Sabbath sleep before I enter the keeping of the whole day. I was delighted to learn recently while staying with new Jewish friends in Miami that some modern Reform Jews also begin their Sabbath celebration at bedtime (but on Friday night instead of Saturday night).

The Jewish custom is to make all the preparations for the coming of the Sabbath Bride before sundown and then at that time to light the Kiddush[5] candles and to welcome the Sabbath Queen. Thus, blissful expectancy marks this ritual that begins the wedding celebration. I have adopted this practice because it decisively begins my Sabbath celebration and sanctifies the day as set apart for a special purpose. After I have completed all my bedtime preparations, the Kiddush ceremony of lighting the candles tangibly marks the moment of ceasing from work. I keep special candles beside my bed (or carry some with me when I travel) and enjoy the candles' glow as I pray an extended prayer beginning

---

5. *Kiddush* literally means "sanctification." In Judaica it is the name for the brief ceremony that ushers in the Sabbath day and that also is performed before all Sabbath or holiday meals (Chaim Grade, *My Mother's Sabbath Days: A Memoir,* trans. Channa Kleinerman Goldstein and Inna Hecker Grade [New York: Alfred A. Knopf, 1986], p. 394). Customarily at sundown on Friday evening two candles are lit—one for the word *observe* and one for the word *remember,* which are used in the two accounts of the Sabbath command in Exodus 20 and Deuteronomy 5. Some Jews celebrate Kiddush just before going to sleep on Friday nights, and some use a single braided candle with two wicks.

with these Jewish phrases: "Blessed art Thou, O Lord our God, King of the Universe, who hast hallowed us by His Commandments and commanded us to kindle the Sabbath light!"[6]

The Jews focus especially on creation in their Kiddush rituals,[7] so I usually spend most of the time thanking God for all his creations in the week that is past and for the Joy[8] of his creating now an opportunity to cease from its labors. I pray about the ways that I will spend the next day and ask that these activities will draw me closer to God and fill me more fully with a sense of his presence in my life. This is also a special time to pray for the Church and for pastors, musicians, and others who contribute to the worship services taking place throughout the world on Sundays. This prayer creates in me a global perspective and provides a weekly preparation so that I can be more ready to worship and less distracted by any thoughts or worries of work.

Obviously, my patterns for beginning the Sabbath are related to my situation as a single person. In *Making Sunday Special*, Karen Burton Mains gives wonderfully extensive suggestions for family observances to begin the Sabbath. (Her family follows the Jewish pattern of beginning Sabbath with the evening meal.) She starts by giving an excellent overview of the following Jewish Sabbath traditions:

1. the lighting of two candles to represent "Observe" and "Remember"

---

6. Mark Zborowski and Elizabeth Herzog, *Life Is with People: The Culture of the Shtetl* (New York: Schocken Books, 1952), p. 43.

7. The Kiddush prayers include thanksgiving for God's creation of light and bread and wine, with which the Sabbath day is begun, and for seedtime and harvest, by which God's creation continues.

8. It is my custom in all my books to capitalize the word *Joy* to emphasize its spiritual nature and to distinguish the deep Joy that comes in one's relationship with God from the more superficial happinesses connected with human circumstances. Joy does not depend on emotions but reflects the will's awareness that all is well when we are God's. See my chapter on Joy in *I'm Lonely, LORD—How Long? The Psalms for Today* (San Francisco: Harper & Row, 1983).

11

2. the Kabalat Shabbat, an ancient evening prayer service of introductory psalms and reference to the creation theme
3. the blessing of the children
4. the singing of "Peace be unto you"—a welcome to the angels
5. the husband's blessing of his wife using words from Proverbs 31:10-31
6. the blessing of the wine using the Kiddush, a prayer of sanctification for the Sabbath
7. the ritual hand-washing and then blessing of the challot, a traditional braided bread
8. the eating and enjoyment of the meal with much laughter and singing
9. the grace when the meal is ended; official closure based on Deuteronomy 8:10
10. the rest of the evening spent in talking to family and friends and in study of the Torah (God's instructions or law).[9]

Next, Mains suggests an order of worship for a Christian "Evening before the Lord's Day" (pp. 32-34). She describes in detail her family's meal on Lord's Day Eve, which includes the lighting of candles, a blessing over the meal, the meal itself with specially planned table conversation, the blessing of the children and spouses, a God Hunt[10] for the children, a God Hunt for the

9. Mains, *Making Sunday Special* (Waco, Tex.: Word Books, 1987), pp. 25-37.
10. The God Hunt, Mains writes, "is the means by which we develop the capacity in ourselves and in our children to recognize God's work in our everyday lives" (p. 48). "Hunting" for examples in these four general categories helps us to see his work:

1. Any obvious answer to prayer
2. Any unexpected evidence of God's care
3. Any unusual linkage or timing
4. Any help to do God's work in the world (*Making Sunday Special*, p. 49)

See also David and Karen Burton Mains, *The God Hunt: A Discovery Book for Men and Women* (Elgin, Ill.: David C. Cook, 1984), and the "God Hunt" discovery book for children, also published by David C. Cook in 1984.

adults (during which time the younger children are excused to play with toys in the Sabbath basket), and prayer in preparation for Sunday (pp. 43-52).

The Mains family holds such meals only monthly—I prefer to begin the Sabbath with a special time of worship every week— but they do a wonderful job of enabling every person to participate in the family worship. I heartily recommend *Making Sunday Special* to you for its many practical ideas for family worship.[11]

Ernest Boyer, Jr., author of *A Way in the World: Family Life as Spiritual Discipline*, suggests these important points for family worship to welcome the Sabbath:

1. Keep it short and simple.
2. Find a way for as many as possible to take part.
3. Do not rely only on words; find simple symbolic gestures to represent the important parts of family life.
4. Come to recognize the power of repetition.
5. Invite others to join you.
6. Have fun.[12]

These ideas provide excellent guidelines for your own creation of the kind of Kiddush rituals that would work best with your family, to help you begin consciously the Sabbath day of ceasing, resting, embracing, and feasting.

I find especially meaningful the Jewish ritual in which the woman of the house moves her arms over the lighted candles in a gesture of embrace to draw to herself "the holiness that rises from their flames." As the representative of her whole household, she draws that holiness not only for herself.[13] I want my own

---

11. Another superb book filled with practical family ideas is Sara Wenger Shenk's *Why Not Celebrate!* (Intercourse, Penn.: Good Books, 1987). Her collection of 150 ideas for worship and celebration includes two liturgies for the Sabbath (pp. 48-52).

12. Boyer, *A Way in the World: Family Life as Spiritual Discipline* (San Francisco: Harper & Row, 1984), pp. 103-5.

13. Zborowski and Herzog, *Life Is with People*, p. 43.

celebrations of the Sabbath to draw the holiness of the day more deeply into my own life as well as into the lives of all those whose lives touch mine. My own Kiddush rituals also include a prayer of relinquishment and a meditation on the angels, represented by two glass angels which glow beautifully in the candlelight and which I welcome with the Jewish greeting, "Peace be unto you, ye ministering Angels, messengers of the most High."[14]

After these rituals, I go to sleep. How rich my sleep always is, because now I have set aside my work for a full twenty-four hours! If, before I fall asleep, I find myself dwelling on aspects of my work (stewing about the book I'm writing or an upcoming speaking engagement), I write down whatever is bothering me on a piece of paper and put it in my study so that I don't have to think about it anymore.

Another aspect of preparation for ceasing work is putting all work materials away as I get ready for the Sabbath. The Jews welcome Queen Sabbath by cleaning the house and preparing the special Sabbath foods so that no cooking needs to be done on the festival day. Similarly, on Saturday nights I stack away all my books and put my writing projects back into baskets and files. In this way I put the work out of mind, too.

During the past few years I spent in graduate school, I couldn't close the door on my work because my computer and all the books for my dissertation were in the living room of my apartment. However, I could at least stack those things up as neatly as possible. I usually spent the Sabbath day away from home or in my kitchen or bedroom so that I wouldn't look at the piles.

Now in my new home in Washington state, I am delighted to have a separate room for my study so that it is easy to shut the door and not look at my work on Sabbath day. It was a great challenge to me on the day I moved in—which was a Saturday— to get all the kitchen things put away and move all the boxes out of the living room into the study so that on Sunday I could celebrate the Sabbath in relative peace. Moreover, it was a test of

---

14. Zborowski and Herzog, *Life Is with People*, p. 45.

my Sabbath convictions not to work at unpacking on that second day in my new home, but I learned a wonderful lesson through the experience. I was so rested by a Sabbath on which I ceased to work that I returned to the unpacking with greater enthusiasm and energy on Monday morning. Ceasing from all our various kinds of work really helps—whether it be dissertation writing, unpacking, housecleaning, or some other task. The Sabbath is a day to abstain totally from whatever is our work at the time.

Jacques Ellul declares that the emphasis on the Sabbath in the Old Testament "shows that work is not after all so excellent or desirable a thing as people often tell us." In our culture, which attaches such a grand importance to work and productivity, our weekly ceasing reminds us that the value of work lies not in itself nor in the worth it gives us, but in the worship of God that takes place in it. The Sabbath, then, is a sign of liberation, Ellul asserts. Jesus never called anyone to work.[15] Rather, Jesus calls each one of us to the vocation of following him and of glorifying God in every dimension of our lives. We will understand this vocation more deeply as we practice Sabbath customs (see Chapter 19).

Our Sabbath keeping is also truly delightful especially because the very process of ceasing from work uncorks our spontaneity and frees our childlike ability to play. Certainly we have all observed that in our society individuals have tremendously deep needs for play. Worries about the stock market and our economic security, fears about climbing the corporate ladder, anxieties about our children or parents or siblings, griefs about our failures and disappointments, frustrations about our limitations, irritations about the state of local or national politics, and despair because of loneliness, bitterness, or communications breakdowns—these things frequently rob us of the delight of play. There is something tremendously freeing about knowing that we don't have any work to do on the Sabbath because we

---

15. Ellul, *The Ethics of Freedom*, trans. and ed. Geoffrey W. Bromiley (Grand Rapids: William B. Eerdmans, 1976), p. 496.

have deliberately set it all aside. This affects every aspect of our existence. In our whole being, we find ourselves free to play.

Suggestions for Sabbath playing will be elaborated throughout these pages, but it is important to note at this point that the freedom to play is a direct result of ceasing work. Obviously, all the concepts of these chapters are intertwined, yet we will build them into a careful progression so that our Sabbath celebrations will be theologically informed, practically possible — and a whole lot of fun.

2. Ceasing Productivity and Accomplishment

ONE OF THE UGLIEST things about our culture is that we usually assess a person's worth on the basis of his or her productivity and accomplishments. One of the first questions we ask when meeting a stranger is "What do you do?" as if the data in the person's response will help us really know who he or she is. Most of our inferiority complexes derive from the fact that we haven't *done* everything we wish to do or that we haven't been as productive as someone else. No matter who we are, we can always find someone who has accomplished more than we have, so we are doomed always to feel second rate.

The need to accomplish also leads to a terrible frenzy about time. (I am always astounded by people whose frenzy forces them to hurry through art galleries. Why come at all if there is no time really to look at, and to be enveloped by, the paintings?) The criterion for everything in our society has become efficiency. We seek power in order to climb the corporate ladder and learn all the tricks of the trade in order to excel. Educational institutions are often dedicated not so much to learning as to academic competition. The root of all of these yearnings to produce is the struggle for security.

17

Trying to accomplish a lot is one of the ways we seek to satisfy the deepest longing of our existence, but inevitably when we reach our goals we will not be satisfied. We will discover that all of our struggle has been, in the words of the preacher of Ecclesiastes, a "chasing after wind" and "vanity of vanities." As the great theologian Augustine acknowledged, "O Lord, thou hast made us, and our spirits are restless until we rest in thee." We will never satisfy the longing for God himself with the accomplishments of our own efforts, so why do we keep trying? And why do we judge the worth of others on the same basis that always leaves us feeling empty?

The second kind of ceasing for which we are freed by the practice of Sabbath keeping is the delight of quitting this endless round of trying to produce. Once we have ceased working, we might as well not feel guilty about it.

When I was preparing for my comprehensive exams in graduate school a few years ago, I had to read at least a book a day in order to prepare everything in my bibliography in the seven months before exams. Then, after passing the exams, I was immediately plunged into the same tempo of reading to prepare for writing my dissertation. As a result of those two years, I developed some very unhealthy notions. After leaving graduate school to return to full-time free-lancing as a Bible teacher and retreat leader, I discovered that I was feeling unsatisfied because I was no longer reading at least a book a day! That probably seems utterly ridiculous to you, but think about what you require of yourself to feel that you have had a "successful" day. Do you need to reach a certain level of accomplishment in order to feel sure that you are a worthwhile person?

One of the largest frustrations often expressed by young mothers is that they feel they are never accomplishing anything when they spend all their time washing diapers or chasing after the toddler who keeps pulling out the kitchen drawers and spilling them all over the floor. Furthermore, the women's liberation movement (among all the good things it has brought about) has done our culture a great disservice by causing many women to feel that if they don't have a career outside the home they cannot be fulfilled. That notion seems to be especially harmful to children in our society; they are made to feel that they are not worth a mother's full-time attention, that it is more important for her to be fulfilled in some sort of career. I long to restore somehow in our culture the sense that raising children is a glorious ministry and career for men as well as women—perhaps the most important one of all. Furthermore, parents raise children primarily by who they *are*, not by what they *do*. I grew up wanting in myself the same love for God and commitment to him that I saw in my parents' dedication and faithfulness.

Setting aside a holy Sabbath means that we can cease our productivity and accomplishments for one day in every seven. The exciting thing about such a practice is that it changes our attitudes for the rest of the week. It frees us up to worry less about how much we produce on the other days. Furthermore, when we end that futile chasing after wind, we can truly rest and learn delight in new ways.

I desperately need to keep Sabbaths faithfully so that this attitude can increasingly pervade the rest of my days; I still get too easily frustrated if I think I have not accomplished enough in a day. During the times I am not able to do very much, I forget that more important things are happening in me as God works to change my character and transform me into his likeness. If I am so worried about my productivity, I usually miss the lessons he is allowing me to experience so that I can be changed.

One of my favorite passages on this topic includes these words of God to Israel:

> But now, this is what the LORD says—
> he who created you, O Jacob,
> he who formed you, O Israel:
> "Fear not, for I have redeemed you;
> I have called you by name; you are mine.
> When you pass through the waters,
> I will be with you;

and when you pass through the rivers,
    they will not sweep over you. . . .
For I am the LORD, your God,
    the Holy One of Israel, your Savior. . . .
Since you are precious and honored in my sight,
    and because I love you . . ." (Isa. 43:1, 2a, 3a, 4a)

Within the context of Yahweh's promises to rescue his people from their captivity and bring the exiles back to their home, this passage focuses on God's overt declarations of what makes his people worthy. Over and over the text insists that Yahweh is the one who makes us valuable. He is the One who created, formed, redeemed, called his people by name, made them his, was with them, protected them, saved them, and made them precious and honored in his sight. The last phrase of this passage is absolutely incredible; the verb that we translate "love" is usually used to denote the love of a husband for his wife. With that kind of personal, intimate love God loves the sinful people of Israel.

God certainly didn't choose Israel because of their accomplishments or their productivity. They were the least among the people of the ancient Near East. They were rebellious and self-centered. They constantly failed to keep up their end of the covenant relationship with Yahweh. So God's love for them is related not to what they do, but to his character as the eternal "I AM."

This is what we celebrate on the Sabbath day. We join the generations of believers—going all the way back to God's people, the Jews—who set aside a day to remember that we are precious and honored in God's sight and loved, profoundly loved, not because of what we produce.

To celebrate God's love on our Sabbaths also transforms us so that we can more deeply value others in the same way. When we are not under the compulsion to be productive, we are given the time to dwell with others, to *be* with them and thereby to discover who they are.

One of my best friends from my years in Indiana is a concert pianist, and I am richly blessed every time I hear her play.

But our frequent Sabbath times together helped me to know her not just for what she accomplishes (which is incredibly wonderful!), but for who she is (which is better yet!). When our productivity was set aside, I experienced her as a person who shares my deepest values, as one who is very sensitive to beauty and cares deeply for others, and as one who is committed to the Lord and to building peace in the world.

Too often we fail to appreciate others because they don't meet our expectations, because they are not as good as we are at certain things, or because they don't measure up to the world's standards for usefulness. It seems to me that the Church could take the lead in suggesting other values by which to cherish individuals. Certainly the One who created and formed us made each of us a unique individual with special attributes. If we can give up our need to produce and to judge others similarly by their accomplishments, we can be freed to value those particular gifts that others bring into our world. Thus, our Sabbath ceasing from productivity can bring great healing into our own lives as well as into the lives of those around us.

Obviously, one of the Sabbath practices that supports this ceasing from productivity is the intentional choice to use time simply to be with people. The point is not necessarily to do anything—perhaps to play, perhaps to share a needed time of gentle affection, but above all simply to be together. We can help each other learn not to find a person's value in his or her accomplishments. Accordingly, one of the greatest gifts of the Christian community can be this nurturing of a better sense of ourselves, a sense not tied in with our usefulness and success. I speak idealistically, of course. It grieves me that our Christian communities get tied into the world's value system and forget this constant message of the Scriptures: that we are worthy because we are loved by God. I hope that you who are reading this book can take the lead in your parishes to cease using productivity as the yardstick by which the value of others is measured.

3. Ceasing Anxiety, Worry, and Tension

JUST LAST SUNDAY I had the privilege of introducing some new materials designed by a denominational insurance company to help families deal with stress. Actually I volunteered to do the presentation for my friend Myron, who was responsible for it, but was too busy writing report cards for his third-grade class to prepare adequately. I wanted to do it—not only to give him a Sabbath gift of freedom from the pressure, but also because the subject ties in well with the whole meaning of the Sabbath, so it gave me a chance to introduce the subject of Sabbath keeping to those present at the meeting.

Consider the statistics on stress in the United States—the phenomenal number of heart attacks that are due to tension and worry, the growing number of stress-related diseases afflicting women as they increasingly enter fields formerly reserved for men, the popularity of exercise clubs to help people reduce the stress in their lives. Just this morning at the pool where I work out I overheard two women talking about the trouble of fitting their exercise programs into their daily schedules; one finally said, "Well, it isn't worth getting all stressed out to make it to the pool in order to relieve the stress."

One of the main causes of modern stress is that we have too much to do. Consequently, Sabbath days—when we don't *have* to do anything—can release us from the anxiety that accompanies our work (as long as we don't add to our stress by taking on too many Sunday responsibilities). Furthermore, our false need to be productive (even in the church) builds stress, especially when we find ourselves unable to meet our exorbitant expectations. We scramble after the security of personal status and think that we will be invincible when we have climbed the corporate ladder and demanded human respect—only to discover our perpetual vulnerability. Thus, our ceasing productivity and accomplishment on Sabbath days is another great stress reliever.

However, it is also necessary to concentrate specifically on ceasing to worry as part of our Sabbath-keeping habits. Several practices help me to set anxiety aside in order to celebrate the Sabbath more thoroughly and to be set more free thereby from anxiety during the other days of the week.

One helpful practice is getting my house ready for "Queen Sabbath." It is important not to let this preparation become an onerous burden in itself; I don't necessarily get the house spotless each Saturday night. But I do enjoy immensely putting away all the projects that feel like work to me. Thus, the Sabbath release from tension begins to happen already on Saturday evenings when I stack up all the business papers and writing projects and books.

The tension drains away more fully as I commit all the things I do for my work into the Lord's hands during the Kiddush prayer at bedtime. If anxiety still continues to plague me after my Sabbath observance has begun, I try to write down my concerns as quickly as possible and as thoroughly as necessary in order to remove the worry from my mind.

Another especially important practice to help me cease worrying is to focus on relationships—particularly my relationship with God—during my Sabbath observance. Instead of status seeking, the day promotes friendship building. In the love of the Christian community we cease being anxious.

23

Other practices will be discussed in the chapters of the three remaining sections of this book, because the Sabbath habits of resting, embracing, and feasting all contribute to our freedom from stress. We are more able to cease worrying when other positive ideas are filling our minds instead.

At this point you might be thinking that it doesn't do any good to set worries aside for just a day. If we merely run away from them, they will be there to bother us the day after the Sabbath. Before I began to practice Sabbath keeping seriously, I too thought that would be the case. On the contrary, I've discovered that the longer I enjoy Sabbaths, the very customs of that day give me not only refreshment, which makes the tension much less powerful in the days that follow, but also new perspectives, new priorities, and a new sense of God's presence, which all cause the tensions themselves to assume a less hostile shape during the week to come. The Sabbath is not a running away from problems, but the opportunity to receive grace to face them.

To keep the Sabbath is a way to practice these verses from Paul's letter to the Philippians:

Rejoice in the Lord always. I will say it again: Rejoice! . . . Do not be anxious about anything, but in everything, by prayer and petition, with thanksgiving, present your requests to God. And the peace of God, which transcends all understanding, will guard your hearts and your minds in Christ Jesus. Finally, brothers [and sisters], whatever is true, whatever is noble, whatever is right, whatever is pure, whatever is lovely, whatever is admirable—if anything is excellent or praiseworthy—think about such things. . . . And the God of peace will be with you. (4:4, 6-8, and 9b)

To celebrate the Sabbath is to rejoice in God's presence. Our practices for the day include extra moments of thanksgiving and special times of prayer and petition, by which we can lay our anxieties and worries before God so that his peace, which both bypasses and surpasses our understanding, can guard our hearts and minds in Christ Jesus. Finally, to think about constructive things rather than our concerns—about beautiful and noble things, that which is excellent and praiseworthy—ushers us into the presence of the God of peace himself.

I love that progression in the Philippians passage. As Paul gives his readers his instructions, including the invitation to put into practice what they had seen and heard in him,[1] he moves them from the experience of God's peace guarding their hearts and minds to the experience of the God of peace being with them. The habits of Sabbath keeping enable us to enjoy that progression more deeply, to know not only the peace of God, but also the presence of God himself. Furthermore, the more we enjoy that experience on Sabbath days, the more easily we can make the progression on more hectic workdays. Our Sabbath customs enable us to practice the presence of God more thoroughly also on days that are not specifically set aside to concentrate on that purpose.

The practice of thanksgiving is one of the best ways I know to cease worrying. However, to understand thanksgiving properly we must first of all combat a dangerous heresy in contemporary Christianity. The false notion that we are to thank God *for* everything has caused immeasurable pain and damage to many Christians.

As one who also suffers from physical impairments, I grieve for many of my handicapped friends who have often been told such things as "You still have your handicaps because you haven't thanked God for them." The heresy specializes in assuring believers that they should ask God for healing just once and then start thanking him for the healing that he is doing. The logical conclusion of such a formulation is that one who isn't healed has not been thanking God properly.

A little bit of exegesis of the Greek phrases in the passages used to support this heresy will clarify the matter. The Philippians passage I just cited stresses that we can "*in* everything . . .

---

1. I omitted the first part of verse 9 from the quotation above in order to emphasize the progression from "the peace of God" to "the God of peace" more clearly.

with thanksgiving" present our requests to God. *In* all our situations we can find reason to thank God—for what he is doing, for how he is with us throughout our troubles, for the ways in which his people have supported us—but we certainly are not commanded to thank God *for* the evils that befall us. I don't thank God *for* the fact that my eyes were burned by radiation and therefore developed cataracts, but I certainly do thank him *in* that situation for the ways in which he has used this handicap to bring about all kinds of good things. I have met many wonderful people in my constant need for transportation. I have seen God's constant provision in the fact that in nine years of free-lance teaching I have never yet lacked a ride to get to my speaking engagements (including an engagement just last week, when two of my usual drivers had conflicts, my next-door neighbor got sick just before I had to leave, and my pastor hurriedly found someone new to take me to the bus station). Certainly I rejoice *in* these gifts of God's goodness, but I do not thank him *for* evil—or else I would never work to combat some of its forms.

Similarly, Ephesians 5:20 in the original Greek says literally that "on behalf of everything" we are to give thanks. Again, that means that we are to thank God not *for* everything, but *in* the midst of everything *on behalf of* what his involvement means. Finally, 1 Thessalonians 5:17 stresses in the same way this careful nuancing of thanking God *in* everything rather than *for* everything.

Our Sabbath days give us the opportunity to find ways to thank God in the midst of our tribulations and anxieties. Many scholars testify that one of the reasons the Jews have remained so strong despite all the afflictions of their history is that they have set aside the Sabbath as a holy day. During the Babylonian captivity, the Sabbath reminded them of their homeland and their God even though they were aliens in a strange land. In the hard times of pogroms in European history, their observance of the Sabbath gave them courage.

I was profoundly moved by the Holocaust Memorial Council's exhibition called "The Precious Legacy: Judaic Treasures from the Czechoslovak State Collections." These treasures were miraculously rescued from destruction during the terrible reign of Hitler because of his intent to study more thoroughly "the Jewish question." Amid the more than 350 religious objects and materials from daily life, the exhibit included pieces revealing that even as captives in concentration camps "Jews turned to religious art as a means of spiritual resistance, creating out of scraps of wood and fabric humble ceremonial objects with which to worship."[2] They used whatever they could find to create Sabbath utensils and prayer garments for themselves so that in the midst of their agony they could celebrate their holy time. The power of Sabbath observance in their lives enabled them to go nobly through terrors that would destroy those of us of lesser faith.

Indeed, when Chaim Grade recounts the moment that he left Vilna to flee the Germans, his mother's last words to him were, "My child, never forget that you are a Jew. Keep the Sabbath." A few days later, exhausted and thirsty, frightened and harassed, he remembered her words, which kept him going.[3]

One of the best ways to cease from anxieties and worries is to recognize our true station in life. Not only do we want to develop Sabbath practices of thanking God, but also we are helped enormously if we stop trying to be God. To that dimension of Sabbath ceasing we turn in the next chapter.

---

2. "The Precious Legacy" by Mark Talisman, Chairman of Project Judaic and Vice-Chairman of the United States Holocaust Memorial Council, New Orleans Museum of Art's *Arts Quarterly* 7 (Jan.-March 1985): 9.

3. Grade, *My Mother's Sabbath Days: A Memoir*, trans. Channa Kleinerman Goldstein and Inna Hecker Grade (New York: Alfred A. Knopf, 1986), pp. 241, 247.

4. Ceasing Our Trying to Be God

ONE OF THE REASONS that the Sabbath is so freeing is that when we cease working, we dispense with the need to create our own future. This was one of the most important lessons taught to the people of Israel during their wilderness experience. When the Sabbath was first becoming an important part of their regular life rhythm, God told them that they would not need to gather manna on the Sabbath day. This account in Exodus is quite exciting:

> Each morning everyone gathered as much as he needed, and when the sun grew hot, it melted away. On the sixth day, they gathered twice as much—two omers for each person—and the leaders of the community came and reported this to Moses. He said to them, "This is what the LORD commanded: 'Tomorrow is to be a day of rest, a holy Sabbath to the LORD. So bake what you want to bake and boil what you want to boil. Save whatever is left and keep it until morning.'"
> So they saved it until morning, as Moses commanded, and it did not stink or get maggots in it. "Eat it today," Moses said, "because today is a Sabbath to the LORD. You will not

find any of it on the ground today. Six days you are to gather it, but on the seventh day, the Sabbath, there will not be any."

Nevertheless, some of the people went out on the seventh day to gather it, but they found none. Then the LORD said to Moses, "How long will you refuse to keep my commands and my instructions? Bear in mind that the LORD has given you the Sabbath; that is why on the sixth day he gives you bread for two days. Everyone is to stay where he is on the seventh day; no one is to go out." So the people rested on the seventh day. (16:21-30)

The point of the whole story is that God will provide for his people; they don't have to struggle to work things out for themselves. Indeed, this is the message throughout the narrative of the Hebrew people—that their God will provide for them. That is the meaning of Holy War—"Stand by and watch the LORD fight for you." He will provide his people with a place to live. He will take them through the Red Sea, across the wilderness, over the Jordan River, and into the Promised Land.

In our twentieth-century spirituality we easily lose the notion of God's provision for us because of our advanced civilization and its distance from the actual processes that provide material goods. A major blessing of Sabbath keeping is that it forces us to rely on God for our future. On that day we do nothing to create our own way. We abstain from work, from our incessant need to produce and accomplish, from all the anxieties about how we can be successful in all that we have to do to get ahead. The result is that we can let God be God in our lives.

This was profoundly reinforced for me while I was writing my dissertation. Six days a week I felt enormous pressure to get the thing done and, later, to be successful in revising it. On Sundays, when I set that work aside, it invariably struck me that I was trying too hard to do everything on my own without trusting God to provide for my future, without sensing his presence in the long hours I spent at the computer. My Sabbath keeping every week put things back into perspective and stirred in me a great repentance for my failure to let God be God in every aspect of my life, especially the academic.

Letting God be God in our lives does not, of course, mean passivity. We do not simply sit back and say that God is in charge of our work. Rather, when we get our priorities straight and remember that God is God and that we are merely his servants, we are empowered to do all that we can to be good stewards of the gifts and resources we have been given. I am convinced that I am freed up to work much better during the times when I am aware of God's direction and provision and empowerment in my daily tasks. Intentional Sabbath ceasing of my striving to be God also makes it more possible for me to think of all the work I do during the week as worship.

In the earliest days of my efforts to keep the Sabbath, I used Sundays to prepare a big pot of stew or soup to last all week so that I wouldn't have to cook while I was busy with my graduate studies. I soon learned, however, that such a practice was spoiling the value of the Sabbath because that activity itself was another attempt to secure my own future. Furthermore, the attitudes engendered while I was cooking were contrary to the purpose of the Sabbath—to free me from all the work that I have to do to provide for myself. Strangely enough, I discovered that when I stopped making the week's pot of stew on Sunday, there was always extra time to do that on another day.

Instead of preparing for the coming week, I could totally enjoy the relaxation of setting work aside. Chapter 25 in Part IV will elaborate on the subject of food. My point here is that my preparation of food for the days ahead was like the Israelites going out to gather manna on the Sabbath or trying to keep it overnight during the week to give themselves some security for the future. The manna turned moldy and became filled with maggots. Similarly, all our stockpiling efforts to create our own future security get pretty wormy when we lose track of God's provision!

The Sabbath is a day to cease striving. We no longer have to scramble after security by trying to be strong, to have all the answers or quick solutions, to be in charge of our time and schedules, to possess controlling authority, or to find easy gratification. What a relief it is not to have to try to be God, nor to create our future, nor to establish our security!

One of the greatest human needs is for security, and we do all kinds of crazy things to try to make sure that we successfully build it. In past times some women married as well as they could (socially) in order to be secure; now the emphasis is on the necessity for women to have lucrative careers so that they can create their own status. We assess various kinds of investments in order to choose the sort that will make us the most secure financially. Our nation builds more and more missiles, bombs, and delivery systems in order to establish our national security—and the ludicrous thing about it all is that this massive nuclear proliferation merely increases the risk that somehow someone will accidentally or angrily push the button and destroy us all.

We also do incredible amounts of personal damage in our striving for security. We manipulate and exploit other people in order to get ahead, to climb the corporate ladder, so that we can be more secure. We are hesitant to be vulnerable, so we hide behind masks in order to remain emotionally secure. Again, all of this is so ridiculous because our very attempts to insure personal security—like our attempts to insure national security—are destructive of it. Professional positions, finances, politics, technological solutions—all are part of the web of illusions that hide from us the fact that our security can be found only in our relationship with God. Professional positions will be eliminated; the stock market might crash; political parties will blunder; technological solutions often create more problems than they solve— but God is eternally the same in his love for us. We can count on his covenant faithfulness.

To face the truth that all our efforts to build security are illusions could lead us to brutal despair if we do not also study the character of God to see how he promises to be our security. Then to cease our striving will lead to the massive relief of totally giving up all our efforts to work things out by ourselves.

31

Similarly, to cease being in control of our own lives leads not to a servile dependence, but to a greater freedom. I would much rather experience the privilege of enjoying to the hilt who I am, seeking to be a faithful steward of my gifts and resources, than try to manage everything by myself. Too many circumstances are out of my control. I can't foretell or change what will happen in the stock market or world economics, what political choices my adversaries or colleagues will make, or what technological procedures will influence my ability to complete what I've planned, so it doesn't do me much good to worry about such things. But if I trust that there is a Lord over all of history—if I recognize that the white horse of Christ rides along with the red horse of war, the black horse of the economy, and the pale horse of affliction and death in controlling the course of history (Rev. 6:1-8)—I can cease to worry about the forces out of my grasp.

My responsibility in living is to be as faithful as I can to my own creation by loving my Creator and his will. That sets me free to enter into the adventure of a daily walk with him, of practicing his presence in all that I do and am becoming.

Throughout the nine years of the existence of C.E.M.— Christians Equipped for Ministry, the corporation under which I free-lance—the board members and I have discovered the delight of letting God be God. (I'm not very good at this, I hasten to admit, but the board members keep trying to help me give up my need to be in control.) We have refused to charge a set fee for my teaching because we want to exercise our faith that if we concentrate on seeking first the kingdom of God, everything else will be added unto us. We have tithed our honoraria because Yahweh has promised that if we tithe he will open the windows of heaven and shower down an abundance of blessings. That does not mean—here I must combat another heresy—that tithing automatically leads to a multiplying of money. In fact, sometimes our treasury has become quite skimpy. But the abundance of blessings has included the Joy both of seeing how God uses our tithes to accomplish his purposes in other ministries and of experiencing his constant provision for all of our ministry's needs.

The greatest demonstration of his provision happened when C.E.M. decided to add another staff person to supervise the ministry in our crisis house, to which we invited women who were homeless or recovering from alcohol or drug abuse or suffering from the agony of divorce. During the entire time that we had another full-time person on the payroll, the honoraria and love offerings I received were adequate for us both. But as soon as our house director resigned, we never again had enough to pay two full-time people. (Nor had we ever had enough for two in the months before she came.) Certainly God's promise bore itself out—that if we sought to do the ministry to which he had called us, he would provide what we needed to accomplish the vision.

In dealing with this subject, we must be careful to understand properly the problem of the millions all over the globe who suffer from the severe economic injustices of our world. Certainly we cannot blame God for the inequities, which are the product of human greed. Moreover, their existence is a profound challenge to all of us who know that God wishes to provide for all his creation, for we are called to be agents of his purposes. Thus, our Sabbath ceasing from our striving to be God invites us instead into positive action as God's servants to confront the materialism of our society, which causes so many in our world to be destitute. Our own materialism is challenged by the importance of trusting God instead of ourselves for our future.

Perhaps this aspect of Sabbath ceasing is especially powerful for me because I have newly experienced the need for such a trust again. During the four years of my graduate program, I received provision for living from fellowships and stipends. That allowed me to forget the delight of seeing how God constantly provides without our needing to be in control. Now that I have returned to full-time free-lancing, I can again experience the thrill of hearing our C.E.M. treasurer tell me that God has graced us again in unexpected ways.

This is just one example that is significant for me in the Sabbath ceasing from striving to be God. I hope that you can apply the idea to your own experience of trying to be in control of your own life. How can a Sabbath practice of ceasing from such attempts better enable you to experience God's provision during the rest of your week? How can the Sabbath habit of noticing how God is our security give you the freedom to stop trying to build it yourself?

When we order our lives around the focus of our relationship with God by letting our Sabbath day be the highlight of our week, toward which everything moves and from which everything comes, then the security of God's presence on that day will pervade the week. One of the customs that helps me to reinforce an awareness of this is the closing ceremony of candle-lighting before I go to sleep on Sabbath night.

The Jews light the Havdalah[1] candles at sundown when the Sabbath ends. Since my Sabbath observance begins at bedtime Saturday, I end it at bedtime Sunday and light candles to say good-bye to the day, just as I lit candles to welcome it the night before. The Jewish Havdalah prayers are filled with longing for the Sabbath to come again, and it is that attitude which has meant so much to me in wanting God to be God in my life. I long for the final consummation of the Sabbath, when God's kingdom will reign supreme and alone. When the final day of this world comes, all of our attempts to be God will be ended in the Joy of his triumphant presence. Meanwhile, if I live each day longing for the special Sabbath day of celebrating his presence, I am much more aware throughout the week that he is with me. Ideally, all the attempts to be in control during the week are thwarted by the consciousness that each moment is leading toward the Sabbath and that each moment also derives its empowerment from the delight of the previous Sabbath.

To live with such an attitude creates a lifestyle with an em-

---

1. *Havdalah* literally means "distinction" or "separation" and is used in Judaica to name the ceremony that marks the end of the Sabbath day and so distinguishes it from the rest of the week, which the ritual ushers in (Chaim Grade, *My Mother's Sabbath Days: A Memoir*, trans. Channa Kleinerman Goldstein and Inna Hecker Grade [New York: Alfred A. Knopf, 1986], p. 393).

phasis that is the opposite of the world's emphasis on productivity as the measure of our worth. It sets believers apart from those who have no need for God, who find themselves sufficient for the tasks of God. For that reason we turn in the next chapter to one of the most common substitutes for God in our culture, and in the chapter after that to the whole question of the Christian community as an alternative to the culture of the society around us.

5. Ceasing Our Possessiveness

THE RELATION OF Sabbath keeping to possessions is an interesting paradox in Judaica. On the one hand, the Jews would choose gladly to live more frugally during the week in order to enjoy the special foods and candles of the Sabbath. On the other hand, the Torah commanded them to refrain from any buying and selling on that day. Thus, both a special appreciation of possessions and a desire not to be dominated by them are part of keeping the Sabbath day holy.

The key to keeping both sides of the paradox together lies in recognizing that the material objects the Jews used for celebrating the Sabbath were just that: not personal possessions, but vessels set apart for the holiness of the day. This is one example of the way in which, especially after the destruction of the Temple, the Jews emphasized the sanctuary of their own homes: they honored the vessels they used for celebrating the Sabbath as holy, even as the vessels used in the Temple services were holy, and the father of the household functioned as the priest for the worship of the home-temple.

This idea corresponds to the New Testament idea of stewardship—that we do not own our possessions, but are instead entrusted with them in order to serve God with them. (See, for example, Paul's words about money in 2 Corinthians 9:11 in Chapter 18 of this book.) How wonderful it would be if in our New Testament homes and temples we could recover the Hebrew sense of sacred possessions.

I have chosen pink candles (since pink is the liturgical color for Joy) for my prayers that begin and end the Sabbath day. Those candles are holy—set apart—for that use only, and, whenever I light them, their gentle glow immediately ushers me into a sense of the Sabbath, the quietness that accompanies the ceasing from work, productivity, anxiety, and striving to control my future, the ceasing that begins when my Sabbath observance commences.

In the same way, I experience a sense of the holy, the set apart, whenever I use my grandmothers' china and silver for dinner parties (which I most often have on Sunday evenings). At first I had trouble justifying my inheritance of all this beautiful china from my mother's mother and silverware from my father's mother. It seemed that I shouldn't enjoy such luxury when so many people in the world are starving. But the Hebrew concept of holy vessels and the added notion of stewardship helped me cast away that false guilt about these possessions. Every time I set the table to welcome guests, I think about my grandparents and give thanks to God for my heritage of their faith and love and commitment. I never would have bought those dishes or that silver, but to use my grandparents' treasures says to my guests that this dinner party is a very holy time, that their special presence in my home calls for the best and most beautiful I can offer, and that God is in the midst of our table fellowship.

On the other hand, the Sabbath is a day to refrain from buying and selling, from acquiring new possessions or additional money. This relates to the idea of not providing for our future on the Sabbath day, as discussed in the previous chapter. Just as the Jews were forbidden to gather manna on the Sabbath, so I have outlawed Sunday errands for myself, having found that it destroys the day's meaning if I go to the grocery store or do other kinds of shopping on Sundays. I really think it is a shame that

our post-Christian culture no longer values the closing of busi-
nesses for the Sabbath, that Sunday is actually one of the most
lucrative days for many stores. I profoundly respect two close
friends of mine who don't open their gas station on Sunday. They
have been faithful to that commitment, and their customers have
continued to patronize their station on weekdays.

The great reformation instituted by Nehemiah after the exiles returned from Babylon to build the walls of Jerusalem included this promise by the people: "When the neighboring
peoples bring merchandise or grain to sell on the Sabbath, we
will not buy from them on the Sabbath or on any holy day" (Neh.
10:31). I wonder how long the people kept that promise.

One of the reasons for refraining from buying or selling on
Sabbath days is that to buy or sell puts the focus on all the wrong
things. We think about what we want instead of what God wants.
We let possessions dominate our desires instead of longing for
the presence of God. (And we might discover, too late, that their
domination becomes almost irrevocable—we become selfish
materialists, gluttons, perhaps even alcoholics or drug abusers.)
Or we focus on what we will get out of a transaction instead of
on the fact that God has given us all our money so that we can
be generous toward others.

That leads to a deeper aspect of the relationship of possessions to the Sabbath, because the day becomes one of giving
things away, of choosing what we do in order to gift others. That
is why I like to have dinner parties on the Sabbath day—especially for those who aren't able to invite me back. I enjoy immensely the giving attitude of a dear Mennonite friend in Indiana; she usually puts extra meat in the pot on Sundays and
invites any worshipers who don't have a place to go to come
home with her family and share their dinner. Wouldn't it be
wonderful if we could recover this custom in our culture—to be
always prepared to welcome the stranger and the sojourner in
our land? (Lev. 19:10, 33-34). (We will discuss Sabbath giving
more fully in Chapter 18.)

On an even deeper level, to refrain from any buying or selling on the Sabbath relates to the day's whole meaning as holy time, which contrasts with the holy space or materialist holiness of religions other than Judaism and Christianity. One of the most profound influences on my appreciation of the Sabbath has been Abraham Joshua Heschel's *The Sabbath*, which begins with this contrast:

> Technical civilization is man's conquest of space. It is a triumph frequently achieved by sacrificing an essential ingredient of existence, namely, time. In technical civilization, we expend time to gain space. To enhance our power in the world of space is our main objective. Yet to have more does not mean to be more. The power we attain in the world of space terminates abruptly at the borderline of time. But time is the heart of existence.
>
> . . . Even religions are frequently dominated by the notion that the deity resides in space, within particular localities like mountains, forests, trees or stones, which are, therefore, singled out as holy places; the deity is bound to a particular land; holiness a quality associated with things of space, and the primary question is: Where is the god? There is much enthusiasm for the idea that God is present in the universe, but that idea is taken to mean His presence in space rather than in time, in nature rather than in history; as if He were a thing, not a spirit.
>
> . . . Judaism is a *religion of time* aiming at *the sanctification of time.* . . .
>
> Judaism teaches us to be attached to *holiness in time.* . . . The Sabbaths are our great cathedrals. . . .
>
> One of the most distinguished words in the Bible is the word *qadosh,* holy; a word which more than any other is representative of the mystery and majesty of the divine. Now what was the first holy object in the history of the world? Was it a mountain? Was it an altar?
>
> It is, indeed, a unique occasion at which the distinguished word *qadosh* is used for the first time: in the Book of Genesis at the end of the story of creation. How extremely significant is the fact that it is applied to time: "And God blessed the seventh *day* and made it *holy.*" There is no

reference in the record of creation to any object in space that would be endowed with the quality of holiness.

This is a radical departure from accustomed religious thinking. The mythical mind would expect that, after heaven and earth have been established, God would create a holy place—a holy mountain or a holy spring—whereupon a sanctuary is to be established. Yet it seems as if to the Bible it is *holiness in time,* the Sabbath, which comes first.[1]

I have quoted Heschel's words at length because no one else can possibly express as wonderfully as he does the significance of holy time, the Sabbath day, instead of holy space, some sort of sanctuary or holy object. In modern Christianity we have totally lost this sense of holy time. We concentrate on our sanctuaries and call those places the church instead of realizing that "church" happens in the events of the Christian community and its outreach to the world, in *time.* We "go to church," meaning a building, and expect to find God there, instead of experiencing the presence of God in the *time* of worship.

That is why it is so important for our Sabbath celebrations to be separated from things, from material possessions, except as they are used to enjoy the time and to experience its holiness—in which case they are valued not for themselves, but simply as means by which God's presence is made more apparent to us. Six days of our week are dominated by the motif of buying and selling, but the Sabbath is a day of giving and ceasing our striving for things. As we keep the Sabbath, instead of our possessing things or space, time possesses us.

---

1. Heschel, *The Sabbath: Its Meaning for Modern Man* (New York: Farrar, Straus & Giroux, 1951), pp. 3, 4, 8, 9 (emphasis Heschel's).

6. Ceasing Our Enculturation

A S WE NOTED in the previous chapter, Abraham Heschel begins his book entitled *The Sabbath* by contrasting our technological civilization and its emphasis on space and the things of space with the religion of Judaism and its emphasis on time. The same contrast should obtain between our culture and Christianity, for Christianity is also composed of holy time and the events that took place in time—the Incarnation, the Crucifixion, the Resurrection, and the coming of the Holy Spirit at Pentecost. Nothing in Christianity supports our contemporary idolatry of space and things, for its God is the same God whose first declaration of *qadosh*, holy, applied to the Sabbath.

Consequently, our observation of the Sabbath is a special time of recognizing that, ideally, as members of the Christian community we are part of an alternative society, standing in contrast to the values of the world and able to offer to those outside the community the opportunity to choose another way. Our ethics are not like those of the world around us; we don't settle for a generalized moral philosophy. Rather, our ethics are shaped by the narrative of our community, the stories of God's interventions in history. Our moral decisions are guided by our focus on

41

time in contrast to a focus on space and things; our relationships with others find their criteria in time and not space.

For the Jewish community, the keeping of the Sabbath day was one of the major marks that set them apart from the world around them. In fact, scholars credit the Jews' observation of the Sabbath with preserving their unique identity during the Babylonian captivity, even as it has continued to preserve Judaica throughout modern Western history. Jewish essayist Achad Haam underlines the vital function of Sabbath tradition in the history of Judaism as follows:

> We can affirm without any exaggeration that the Sabbath has preserved the Jews more than the Jews have preserved the Sabbath. If the Sabbath had not restored to them the soul, renewing every week their spiritual life, they would have become so degraded by the depressing experiences of the workdays, that they would have descended to the last step of materialism and of moral and intellectual decadence.[1]

At one point Reform Jews even debated whether or not they should observe the Sabbath on Sunday instead of Saturday in order to fit in better with the surrounding culture, but that proposal was soundly defeated. They have always observed the Sabbath on the seventh day, and they shall always do so.

The earliest Christians at first celebrated both the Sabbath on the seventh day (Saturday), in keeping with their Jewish heritage, and the Lord's Day on the first day of the week (Sunday), in keeping with their recognition that Christ's resurrection was the major turning point for their faith. The Jews emphasized a Sabbath of resting and thinking about God's creation and deliverance, a seventh day of delight serving as a sign of the covenant. To all of this the Christians added their remembrance of the radical reorientation of the Sabbath that Jesus demon-

---

1. Haam, quoted by Karen Burton Mains, *Making Sunday Special* (Waco, Tex.: Word Books, 1987), p. 25.

strated, especially in his healing miracles on that day, and they
also set apart the day of his resurrection to celebrate his continu-
ing Lordship.

It seems that Sunday became the exclusive day for worship
only after persecution in Jerusalem dispersed the Christians and
caused Christianity's great expansion among the Gentiles. The
change was legislated by an edict on Sunday observance issued
by the Emperor Constantine in C.E. 321.[2] The great misfortune of
the change, however, is that in the process Christianity lost its
sense of the importance of keeping the Sabbath day holy. Why
is it that we pay great attention to the commandments not to mur-
der and steal (and think those are terrible sins), but don't recognize the significance of our failure to obey the commandment to
observe the Sabbath day?

Increasingly in our culture, the Ten Commandments do not
provide the moral foundation for society. The commandment to
worship God and him only was the first to be lost, but now, to
a tragic extent, our culture no longer respects the commands to
honor parents and not to commit adultery. Many people wonder
how these outdated commandments can matter in a twentieth-
century world. In fact, the commandments as a clear basis for
morality are desperately needed more than ever in our fragmented, disrespectful, violent, covetous society.

It seems to me that to recover the command to keep the Sabbath might help our Christian communities to restore the other
commandments. Certainly if we honor one day as a day set apart
to concentrate on the holiness of God, our priorities will be restored, and we will again seek God's will concerning our relationships with parents, with sexual partners, and with possessions.

We already set ourselves apart from the surrounding culture

---

2. In this book I use the terms B.C.E. (Before the Common Era) and
C.E. (Common Era) instead of the customary B.C. (Before Christ) and A.D.
(Anno Domini—"in the year of our Lord") to be consistent with my in-
tention to value the contributions of Jewish thought for their own sake
and not only as they prefigure Christ. That is also why I refer to the
"Hebrew Scriptures" rather than to the "Old Testament."

when we choose not to work in any way on the Sabbath. We further extricate ourselves from society's values if we give up the need for accomplishment and abstain from worry and anxiety about our position. We choose deliberately to be different from our culture if we give up our striving to be God and let Yahweh be God instead. We definitely do not conform to our culture if we choose not to be dominated by possessions or by the anxiety to acquire more of them, but decide instead to give away much of what we have and use what we have been given as good stewards who desire to enjoy the things of God for the purposes of God.

We could list many other ways to keep the Sabbath that ideally could set the Christian community apart as an alternative society to the surrounding culture. I'd like to focus on one particular dimension that may surprise you in this book—our personal sexuality.

I am writing here not about genital sexuality, but about social sexuality in the sense of how we relate to each other as men and women (and not as partners in intercourse).[3] Partly because of our society's mad rush to meet deeper emotional needs by frantic abuse of genital sexuality, which was designed by God to be enjoyed only within the framework of a committed covenantal relationship, there is much confusion in our culture about our social sexuality. We are confused about what it means to be men and women, about what masculinity and femininity are in themselves and in the fullness of intimate relationships that are godly. In addition, in the attempt to end gender discrimination, we have—unfortunately—largely lost many genuine values of our masculinity and femininity.

It is significant that in the same account which ends with God's calling the seventh day holy and which establishes forever the sacredness of the Sabbath (see the discussion in the previous chapter) we also find the most profound passage about our masculinity and femininity. This is the description Genesis 1-2 offers:

---

3. See a complete explication of this differentiation in Joyce Huggett's *Dating, Sex, and Friendship* (Downers Grove, Ill.: InterVarsity Press, 1985).

Then God said, "Let *us* make *humankind* in *our* image, in *our* likeness, and let *them* rule *with* the fish of the sea and the birds of the air, *with* the livestock, *with* all the earth, and *with* all the creatures that move along the ground."

So God created *humankind* in his own image,
in the image of God he created him;
male and *female* he created them.

. . . God saw all that he had made, and it was *very* good. And there was evening, and there was morning—the sixth day. Thus the heavens and the earth were completed in all their vast array.

By *the seventh day* God had finished the work he had been doing, so on *the seventh day* he rested from all his work. And God blessed *the seventh day* and made it *holy*, because on it he *ceased* from all the work of creating that he had done. (Gen. 1:26-27, 31 and 2:1-3, translation and emphases mine)

Several points in this text require careful consideration.

First, the necessarily close connection of the sixth and seventh days would imply that human beings, whom God made in his image on the sixth day, will be faithful to that image by resting and ceasing on the seventh day, even as God did. That was the understanding throughout the development of Jewish faith, for the commandment to honor the Sabbath in the Exodus account stresses this dimension of creation and our imitation of God in his resting.

Second, God created human beings in his own image, an image which, among other things, specifically focuses on relationship. God says, for example, "Let *us* make *humankind* in *our* image, in *our* likeness."[4] We bear the image of God in our relating to one another as males and females.

Closely connected with the preceding is the awareness that to fulfill one's greatest potential as a human being is to reflect the

---

4. I originally learned this idea from Paul K. Jewett's *Man as Male and Female: A Study in Sexual Relationships from a Theological Point of View* (Grand Rapids: William B. Eerdmans, 1975).

image of God, which is reflected in one's own unique maleness or femaleness. We have learned from the works of modern psychologists such as Jung that each of us is composed of various elements formerly ascribed to masculinity or femininity. We search in others for what we lack in our own *animus* and *anima*. Long before these insights were developed, however, this text had set us free to define our particular femininity or masculinity as the way in which each of us shows the picture of God. It doesn't matter that in our culture's stereotypes certain leadership attributes in my character were formerly thought of as masculine traits; if they are ways in which the image of God is displayed in me, then those attributes are part of my being a woman in the likeness of God. Since God is neither male nor female, but more than that, and yet condescends to reveal something of himself by the way we are created in his image, we can each rejoice in the way in which our particular personalities, housed in our femaleness or maleness, reflect a bit of who God is.

Furthermore, since the Sabbath day is the holy time in which I seek to know God better and to focus on his presence in my life, that becomes a special day in which I discover new dimensions of my femaleness as it reflects the image of God. The same is true, of course, for all my devotional times, but to keep the Sabbath involves a special concentration on God so that the whole day can be filled with such discovery. The better I know God, the better I can know how my own femininity displays his likeness.

On a Sabbath-day walk this fall in Wisconsin, for example, I discovered an important dimension of my own femininity. It seemed strange, but as I walked along and noticed all the cotton puffs of milkweed in the fields, I was overcome by a great longing for their softness—softness that is largely shut out by our technological society and by the scholarly world in which I had spent most of my time in recent years. I culled the cloudy fibers from several pods by the roadside and held them against my face for a few miles as I walked. As I reflected on my deep longing for more softness in my life, I realized that the source of such longing lies in my human yearning for God. That awareness, in turn, led me to think about how God is soft—tender, compassionate, forgiving, healing, providing, comforting, nursing—and how I could in my own peculiar ways imitate his softness. (These reflections, of course, are not meant to negate other aspects of God's character, such as his justice and holiness, which cause him to function as a Judge and a Warrior. God's innumerable attributes and actions always invite us to discover new dimensions of his infinite revelation of himself.)

God's softness and the ways in which his people can extend it to others were important concepts for me to grasp that day because I don't usually think of myself as soft. I usually have to be the strong one in charge, the one with answers, the teacher. But for the last few years I've been gradually discovering and learning to concentrate on how I can be a healer, a source of softness.

Think for a minute about the last time you discovered something new in your own personality—how it freed you to be able to express some aspect of yourself that previously lay hidden, how it thrilled you to be truly yourself in your relationship with others or another in particular. Such discoveries enable us to be more truly the women and men God created us to be.

For me this is one of the particular delights of the Sabbath, for when I set aside the values of the culture around me—its roles and expectations, its definitions of what it means to be a woman—and focus instead on who God is and how I'm created in his image, I learn all sorts of new things about my own femininity. Ceasing to value what the culture expounds sets me free to be more truly myself as a woman formed to reflect the character of God in my own unique ways.

We could choose many other examples of our deliberate Sabbath rejection of the ideas of our culture, but this particular aspect of refusing to conform to our society's understanding of our sexuality demonstrates the principle, which will unfold in many of the other chapters of this book. An especially important matter is the follow-up of this ceasing: we must embrace a different set of values. We will turn to that positive side of the topic in Chapter 16.

7. Ceasing the Humdrum and Meaninglessness

ONE OF THE WORST PROBLEMS for those who don't observe the Sabbath day is that life can become so humdrum, every day the same—day after day! The pressures of work never let up; there is *always* something more to do. Our culture's great need to cease working is evidenced by the mass exit from the cities for the weekend—thousands of people are trying to "get away from it all." The ironic thing is that these attempts usually cannot be successful because most of those trying to run away from the pressures of their work aren't actually doing anything to relieve those pressures or lessen their anxieties. Merely to run from work, productivity, tensions, striving to be in control, the hassles of buying and selling, and the prevailing cultural values doesn't work because one must come back to them again.

Celebrating the Sabbath is different from running away. We do not merely *leave* the dimensions discussed in the preceding six chapters—we actually *cease* letting them have a hold on our lives.

Everything is turned around when we keep the Sabbath. If we don't observe it, Sunday just leads us back into the humdrum of the regular workweek (which leaves a great number of people awfully depressed on Sunday evenings); keeping the Sabbath ushers us into the recognition that all days derive their meaning from the Sabbath. As Abraham Heschel points out, the spirit of the Bible is different from that of Aristotle, who asserted that "'relaxation . . . is not an end'; it is 'for the sake of activity,' for the sake of gaining strength for new efforts." Heschel continues,

> To the biblical mind, however, labor is the means toward an end, and the Sabbath as a day of rest, as a day of abstaining from toil, is not for the purpose of recovering one's lost strength and becoming fit for the forthcoming labor. The Sabbath is a day for the sake of life. Man is not a beast of burden, and the Sabbath is not for the purpose of enhancing the efficiency of his work. "Last in creation, first in intention," the Sabbath is "the end of the creation of heaven and earth."
>
> The Sabbath is not for the sake of the weekdays; the weekdays are for the sake of Sabbath. It is not an interlude but the climax of living.[1]

In our American culture, in which every person is judged by his or her work and rest is determined by our labors, we desperately need this radical reorientation, made possible by the Jewish concept of time in which rest determines work. Such a concept reorients our entire way of thinking about people, as we will see especially in Chapter 14.

The fact that Jews organize life around the Sabbath is well demonstrated by a book called *My Mother's Sabbath Days*. The author, Chaim Grade, organizes his memories of life before, during, and after the Holocaust by means of bits of stories about his mother's Sabbath observances. Although he himself does not

---

1. Heschel, *The Sabbath: Its Meaning for Modern Man* (New York: Farrar, Straus & Giroux, 1951), p. 14. His quotations are from Aristotle's *Ethica Nicomachea* X, 6; Rabbi Solomo Alkabez's *Lechah Dodi* (the Kiddush hymn referred to in Chapter 1); and the Evening Service for the Sabbath.

follow in the ways of her piety, he is powerfully molded by the centrality of Sabbath keeping in his childhood home.[2]

To return to Sabbath keeping is not nostalgia or an attempt to return to an age that is pre-Enlightenment, pre-Industrial Revolution, and pre-Darwinian. Rather, it is a return to the spiritual dimension that haunts us. In an age that has lost its soul, Sabbath keeping offers the possibility of gaining it back. In an age desperately searching for meaning, Sabbath keeping offers a new hope. In contrast to the technological society, in which the sole criterion of value is the measurement of efficiency,[3] those who keep the Sabbath find their criteria in the character of God, in whose image they celebrate life.

The delight of the Sabbath and its resting, embracing, and feasting give new energy and meaning to life as its climax and focal point. We will explore these positive aspects in the following sections of this book.

---

2. Grade, *My Mother's Sabbath Days: A Memoir,* trans. Channa Kleinerman Goldstein and Inna Hecker Grade (New York: Alfred A. Knopf, 1986). I also recommend this book highly for the purpose of Christians' gaining a better understanding of the immensity of the destruction of the Holocaust for Jewish people. We must recognize the cost not only in the lives of six million Jews, but also in the agony and questioning of those who survived. See especially pp. 367-71 of Grade's book, in which he describes searching the ruins of the Vilna ghetto for some sort of comprehension when everything argued only for the injustice of the world.

3. See particularly the works of Jacques Ellul on this theme—especially *The Technological Society* and *The Technological System.*

PART II
RESTING

By the seventh day God had finished the work he had been doing, so on the seventh day he rested from all his work.

—Genesis 2:2

The spiritual rest which God especially intends in this commandment [to keep the Sabbath holy] is that we not only cease from our labor and trade but much more—that we let God alone work in us and that in all our powers do we do nothing of our own.

—Martin Luther

SECOND MEANING of the Hebrew verb *shabbat* is "to rest." In the Hebrew Scriptures to desist from labor is associated with resting—for God, people, animals, even the land. In this section we will look at various aspects of Sabbath rest (spiritual, physical, emotional, intellectual, and social), at aids to Sabbath rest, and at the significance of resting according to an ethics of Christian character.

We might wonder how anyone can possibly truly rest when there is so much to do. As we will discover in this section, an added benefit of a day of complete physical rest is that it gives us extra strength and zeal for the tasks of the other six days. Moreover, a day especially set aside for worship teaches us to carry the spirit of worship into our work. Furthermore, to give ourselves a day's break from emotional and intellectual problems enables us to come back to them with fresh perspectives, creative insights, and renewed spirits.

To have already deliberately set apart a whole day for rest makes "the choice to rest" easier, because the discipline of observing the Sabbath has reoriented our entire week's calendar. In fact, the Hebrew days of the week don't even have independent names but are named in relation to the Sabbath. So, for example, Sunday is called "the first day to the Shabbat."[1] In her book entitled *Making Sunday Special,* Karen Burton Mains stresses that if the Sabbath is the high point of the week, we spend three days getting ready (preparing for the bride) and three days afterward remembering it (the delight of the wedding). She diagrams such a "rhythm of the sacred" with this calendar:

---

1. David and Karen Burton Mains, "The Sacred Rhythm of Work and Play," *Moody Monthly,* June 1985, p. 18.

Anticipation	Celebration	Reflection
the "Observe"		the "Remember"
of Deut. 5:12		of Exod. 20:8
Thursday, Friday, Saturday	Sunday	Monday, Tuesday, Wednesday[2]

The more persistently we practice the discipline of preparing for the Sabbath in the three days preceding it, and the more thoroughly we enjoy its benefits in the three days following it, the more delightfully restful the Sabbath itself will be for us in its actual practice, as well as in its anticipation and remembrance as these transform the entire week.

Furthermore, each kind of resting plays an important part in the working together of the whole. Just as true resting from work is more than ceasing to work, so the complete resting of our whole being is more than mere physical rest without labor. To rest utterly in the grace of God is the foundation for wholistic rest.

---

2. Mains, *Making Sunday Special* (Waco, Tex.: Word Books, 1987), pp. 21, 104-5.

8. Spiritual Rest

ALTHOUGH PHYSICAL REST is the first dimension that readily comes to mind when we think of Sabbath rest, we can't begin immediately with that aspect because it is really impossible to rest our bodies thoroughly if our spirits are ill at ease. In the previous section we recognized that if we ceased work on the Sabbath day we could also give up the whole attitude of productivity, the worries associated with that pressure, our striving to be in control of our lives, our scrambling for possessions, and our entrapment in our culture and the resultant meaninglessness and boredom. In the same way, we will see in this section that various kinds of resting form a progression— beginning with the spiritual.

We must discuss that dimension of resting first because we can truly learn how to rest only when we are genuinely freed by God's grace. Our Sabbath observance will not give us genuine rest if we use it merely as an excuse to be workaholics the rest of the week. Only in the sure knowledge that we don't have to manufacture our success in life by our own efforts can we have the freedom not to be continuously working at making our own way. Redemption of the spirit releases us

55

and calls us away from the struggles of the heart. Grace, indeed, lets us rest in peace.

This relates closely to our previous discussion in Chapter 4 about letting our future lie in God's hands. When we cease striving to be God, we learn a whole new kind of contentment, the delight of the presence of God in our present circumstances. When we give up our silly rebellion against God's purposes, we discover that he provides the security for which we were searching.

The progression from ceasing to resting underscores the basic movement from idolatry to faith. First we discover all the deception and falsehood of the securities offered by the world, and, with repentance, we *cease* to trust them. This includes especially all of our efforts to make our own way or to save ourselves. Then we learn that God has done all the work of redemption for us and that he continues to work through us. We learn, by faith, to *rest* in his grace.

This was the major discovery of the Reformation. Martin Luther stressed the importance of spiritual rest in his "Treatise on Good Works" as follows:

> The spiritual rest which God especially intends in this commandment [the covenant command to keep the Sabbath holy] is that we not only cease from our labor and trade but much more—that we let God alone work in us and that in all our powers do we do nothing of our own.[1]

Luther then emphasizes that human beings are totally corrupted by sin and underscores the possibility of crucifying that nature in Christ (Gal. 5:24) so that God can work through us in good works of "fasting, watching, [and] labor." The two steps of the first two sections of this book are underscored by Luther's proclamation "that our works cease and that God alone works in us" as we rest.[2]

---

1. Luther, "Treatise on Good Works," in *The Christian in Society* I, trans. W. A. Lambert, rev. James Atkinson, vol. 44 of *Luther's Works*, gen. ed. Helmut T. Lehmann (Philadelphia: Fortress Press, 1966), p. 72.

2. Luther, "Treatise on Good Works," p. 73.

The value of a day set apart for remembering God's grace has always been part of the Jewish Sabbath traditions. As I read through the *Sabbath and Holiday Prayer Book,* I was profoundly moved by the great emphasis on grace, repentance, and the goodness of God (sounding very much like Martin Luther!) in all the liturgies and prayers.[3] Matitiahu Tsevat, a scholar of the Hebrew Scriptures, insists that the basic meaning of the biblical Sabbath is an "acceptance of the sovereignty of God." We always try to be in control of our lives, but the seventh-day observance reminds us that God is the master of time. In its opportunity for reflection, the Israelite "renounces his autonomy and affirms God's dominion over him."[4]

One of the necessary tools for spiritual resting is the Word of God. The Torah[5] was the focus of the Sabbath for the Jews, who spent part of the day immersed in the study of it. For Christians, the entire canon of Hebrew and Christian Scriptures teaches us about God's covenant love—as we both privately read and meditate upon it in our personal Sabbath devotions and publicly hear it proclaimed and preached upon in our corporate worship (an essential aspect of Sabbath keeping which is the focus of Chapters 22 and 23). By means of God's Word we set our minds and spirits upon heavenly things and set aside our daily business in order to rest in the grace of God.

The creation account in Genesis establishes the pattern for time by naming a day as evening followed by morning rather than morning followed by evening. According to Eugene Peterson, pastor and writer,

---

3. S. Singer, *Sabbath and Holiday Prayer Book,* English trans. (New York: Hebrew Publishing, 1926).

4. Tsevat, "The Basic Meaning of the Biblical Sabbath," in *The Meaning of the Book of Job and Other Biblical Studies: Essays on the Literature and Religion of the Hebrew Bible* (New York: Ktav, 1980), pp. 49, 48.

5. The Hebrew word *torah* is usually translated "law," but a better rendering for understanding its implications is the term "instruction." The first five books of the Bible are officially designated the Torah because they contain God's laws for his covenant people, but the name is sometimes applied generally to the entire corpus of the Hebrew Scriptures.

[This] Hebrew evening/morning sequence conditions us to the rhythms of grace. We go to sleep, and God begins his work. As we sleep he develops his covenant. We wake and are called out to participate in God's creative action. We respond in faith, in work. But always grace is previous and primary. We wake into a world we didn't make, into a salvation we didn't earn.

Evening: God begins, without our help, his creative day. Morning: God calls us to enjoy and share and develop the work he initiated.[6]

The first creation account then concludes by setting apart the seventh day as a special day for rest. Thus, the rhythm of evening/morning grace and work is enfolded in the larger rhythm of a Sabbath set apart to focus on grace and six days of work within that grace. This sense of beginning with grace is the reason that I begin my Sabbath observance when I go to bed on Saturday night. In the rest of sleep I experience a fundamental undergirding of grace.

In *The Sabbath* Abraham Heschel talks about spiritual rest in terms of the Hebrew word *menuha*. That word, usually rendered "rest," means "much more than withdrawal from labor and exertion, more than freedom from toil, strain or activity of any kind." Rather than a negative concept, the word connotes "something real and intrinsically positive." The ancient rabbis believed that "it took a special act of creation to bring it into being, that the universe would be incomplete without it."[7] The *Genesis rabba*, a rabbinic commentary on Genesis, asks what was created on the seventh day. Its answer is "Tranquility, serenity, peace and repose."[8]

All these words create images not merely of physical resting, but of the resting of my whole being, the true me. I long for more of such trusting rest in my life and know that it is thwarted

---

6. Peterson, "The Pastor's Sabbath," *Leadership*, Spring 1985, p. 53.
7. Heschel, *The Sabbath: Its Meaning for Modern Man* (New York: Farrar, Straus & Giroux, 1951), pp. 22-23.
8. *Genesis rabba* 10:9.

whenever my relationship with God is not central. Every time I rely on my own efforts or choose other gods, I block the serenity and peace that God freely gives. I think again of Saint Augustine's famous phrase, "O, Lord, thou has made us, and our spirits are restless until we rest in thee."

Heschel's discussion of *menuha* continues as follows:

> To the biblical mind *menuha* is the same as happiness and stillness, as peace and harmony. . . . It is the state in which there is no strife and no fighting, no fear and no distrust. The essence of good life is *menuha*. "The Lord is my shepherd, I shall not want, He maketh me to lie down in green pastures; He leadeth me beside the still waters" (the waters of *menuhot*). In later times *menuha* became a synonym for the life in the world to come, for eternal life.
>
> Six evenings a week we pray: "Guard our going out and our coming in"; on the Sabbath evening we pray instead: "Embrace us with a tent of Thy peace."[9]

Many of Heschel's comments are important for our understanding of the nature of the spiritual rest that is experienced in Sabbath keeping.

In the first place, he describes Sabbath rest as peace. The Hebrew word *shalom*, which we translate "peace," means, most importantly, "peace with God." If we are not at peace with God, no other kind of true peace is possible. As Christians we know that reconciliation with God has been made possible by the atoning work of Jesus Christ. I love Paul's proclamation in 2 Corinthians that "if anyone is in Christ, *there is* a whole new creation."[10] That means that everything has changed! When we have been reconciled to God, all kinds of things are different. This accentuates the point that biblical peace is not a passive condition or state of being, but really an exciting process. As Paul stresses, God's work to reconcile us through the suffering and death of Christ

---

9. Heschel, *The Sabbath*, pp. 22-23.
10. 2 Corinthians 5:17. This translation was first suggested to me by John Howard Yoder.

also thereby makes us ambassadors of reconciliation. The freedom we experience because our sins are not counted against us makes us eager to carry that message of forgiveness to the world.

When we celebrate the resting of Sabbath keeping, we become immersed more deeply in this peace of God, this awareness that all the barriers have been broken down. As a result, we are empowered to work to break down the barriers that divide the world around us, and we can experience the *menuha* Heschel describes—harmony, a state of being without strife, fighting, fear, or distrust. (See the development of this idea in Chapter 13.)

I was overcome by a deep feeling of repose when I first read Heschel's words about the "waters of *menuhot*" in connection with Psalm 23. How much that psalm is loved by believers of all ages, but how rarely we truly understand the depth of comfort that it offers! Our shepherd Lord not only provides for our physical nourishment by taking us to green pastures, but also enfolds us in contentment and tranquility by leading us beside the waters of stillness. Those words promise us profound solace for our spirits. We have probably all gazed at incredibly calm pools or peaceful ponds in silent forests or quiet meadows and felt their stillness enter into our souls. Another image that conveys such rest is the picture of a child being held securely in a parent's arms and cradled gently in a rocking chair.

I don't usually experience such enfolding. Being a middle-aged single woman who is not really rooted in a community because my work involves so much travel, I often long for the kind of parental or spousal cherishing that would enfold me and say, "There, there—it will be all right!" So many times when I feel I have to fight all my battles alone, I wish I could crawl onto someone's lap to be held and stilled.

Perhaps you identify with those feelings. It seems to me that one of the deepest needs in our technologized, and therefore non-intimate, society is the need for the tranquility of spirit that the "waters of *menuhot*" imply.

God's enfolding rest and peace descended upon me once in an astonishing measure. In the middle of writing my dissertation, I was feeling horribly overwhelmed by it all. One afternoon one of my favorite pieces of music, Ralph Vaughan Williams' *Variations on a Theme by Thomas Tallis*, came on the radio just when I'd reached a point of exhaustion and despair. I ceased working, settled into my beanbag chair (so dilapidated that it enfolds me), and listened to the piece undisturbed.

During those weeks I had also been studying W. Bingham Hunter's *The God Who Hears* in my quiet time and trying to relate to God more as "Abba."[11] As the lush harmonies of the strings playing Vaughan Williams' music moved me to the emotional breaking point, the thought of God as a tender father holding me on his lap suddenly flooded my imagination. I felt the security of being enfolded, yet the gentleness of a grasp not too tight. I was not controlled, but set free; understood, yet not so vulnerable that I could be crushed. I was held, and, in the love of that embrace, I wept in relief.

It was a rest more deep than any other I have ever known, and since that time I have come closest to experiencing such rest again on Sabbath days. On days set apart to focus on who God is, his gifts of rest and peace are most likely to be experienced. Indeed, the possibility for that first enfolding moment was created by a Sabbath ceasing from work and resting in Vaughan Williams' exquisite melodies and harmonies, which ushered me into the very presence of God himself.

The greatest result of Sabbath resting is the opportunity to know the presence of God, no matter what our present circumstances might be. We do not need to rely on our own strength to deal with the tragic. Rather, spiritual rest gives us the freedom to accept the fact that human happiness is fleeting and to trust that there will be enough grace to carry us through all tragedy. We might be experiencing a time of sadness and mourning, but our faith assures us that God is with us in our sorrow to bring us the Joy of his presence.

---

11. Hunter, *The God Who Hears* (Downers Grove, Ill.: InterVarsity Press, 1986), especially pp. 96-99.

Instead of categorizing everything (especially God) into neat little boxes limited to our own finite understanding, we are given the ability to live with paradox, to have faith in what we cannot see, to deal constructively with the tensions of contradictions. In short, spiritual rest enables us to let God be God. When we cease from all our labors to control or to understand, there is time in our space for the eternal.

Sabbath resting is a foretaste of eternal life. Someday we shall know this rest, this *menuha*, in its fullness. For that reason, part of our Sabbath celebration is a prayer that we might someday come to the fulfillment of the Sabbath. This grows especially strong for me during the Advent season. On the first Sunday of Advent I always put up my angel choir and manger scene (without the Christ Child in it yet) to remember again what it means that Jesus came the first time, to repent that I'm never ready for his coming and that I always lose track of his presence in my daily life, and to anticipate, and yearn for, his coming again.

Some of that yearning can blessedly be a part of all our Sabbath celebrations. The Jews bid good-bye to the Sabbath with final prayers that include a pang of longing for its next appearance seven days later. When we live for our Sabbaths, when they are the climax of our weeks, we know a healthy anticipation of the ultimate rest, the time when Jesus will come to take us home.

The very word *home* conveys a bushel of feelings, doesn't it? The sound of the word itself conveys comfort and tenderness and security and the freedom to be oneself. Recently, even deeper feelings about "home" were stirred up in me because for five months I was without one. Last May I moved from my home in Indiana because I had so many commitments to teach at camps and various conferences until the end of October that it was wasteful stewardship to pay rent for an apartment in which I would never be. As the months dragged on, however, I became painfully aware of how desperately I needed a desk to stay organized, how deeply I missed certain books in my library for Bible-study preparations, how profoundly I wanted to be at my computer to write, how greatly I longed to be able to invite friends over for a Sabbath dinner party.

Now at last I have a home again, and some nights the bedtime prayer "Oh, God, I love my new home!" just bursts out. My spirit overflows with contentment and gratitude to be home at last. This present happiness, however, is just a foretaste of the true Joy that will be mine when I finally go home.

A growing number of people in the United States are winding up on the streets because they have no home at all. Their tragic plight illustrates the broken character of our world, how cockeyed it is because of sin. They have a right to resent the injustice of the world and to be angry about their circumstances. Others might experience a feeling of homelessness even though they live in expensive houses because they don't feel that they really belong anywhere. Some might feel homesick because they can never go back to the childhood home they dearly loved. These and various other needs and desires give rise to great yearnings for a home. These deep longings help us to appreciate more the immensity of the hope we have in Christ that some day we will truly go home. How desperately we all need our true home, where we can freely be ourselves, certainly know that we are secure, and Joyfully experience the presence of God face to face.

Sabbath keeping is one way to anticipate our going home and, in part, to experience its Joys even now. (This eschatological understanding of the Sabbath will be elaborated in Chapter 22.) As Heschel teaches us, the Sabbath prayers are different from those of ordinary days in which we ask God to guard our going out and our coming in. On the Sabbath instead we ask God to embrace us with the tent of his peace. That image is extraordinarily powerful throughout the Scriptures because it connotes the presence of God in a very special way. When the earliest people of Israel wandered in the wilderness, their tent of God's presence was particularly visited with Yahweh's glory (see Exod. 40:34-38, as well as Ezek. 10:1-22 and 43:4-9). Furthermore, in the incarnation of Jesus, God "pitched his tent and dwelt among us, full of grace and truth" (a literal translation of John 1:14).

Finally, at the end of the Scriptures, in the Book of Revelation, we are promised that at the end of time "he who sits on the throne will spread his tent" over his people (Rev. 7:15b).

In our Sabbath prayers, then, we request the profound rest of God. We ask him to embrace us with the tent of his peace, the very dwelling of his presence.

9. Physical Rest

THE STORY IS TOLD of a wagon train on its way from St. Louis to Oregon. Its members were devout Christians, so the whole group observed the habit of stopping for the Sabbath day. Winter was approaching quickly, however, and some among the group began to panic in fear that they wouldn't reach their destination before the heavy snows. Consequently, several members proposed to the rest of the group that they should quit their practice of stopping for the Sabbath and continue driving onward seven days a week.

This proposal triggered a lot of contention in the community, so finally it was suggested that the wagon train should split into two groups—those who wanted to observe the Sabbath and those who preferred to travel on that day. The proposal was accepted, and both groups set out and traveled together until the next Sabbath day, when one group continued while the other remained at rest.

Guess which group got to Oregon first.

You're right. The ones who kept the Sabbath reached their destination first. Both the people and the horses were so rested by their Sabbath observance that they could travel much more vigorously and effectively the other six days of the week. God honors those who honor his commands.

Someone told me that historical story so long ago that I can't remember where it came from or if I have all the details correct. But the story was so exciting to me many years ago (I've been thinking about this Sabbath book for a *long* time) that I have never forgotten it. The principle it propounds has proved true in my own life, especially during the last four years, when I was working on my doctorate. Some of my classmates teased me that I would never get my work done if I continued to refrain from studying on Sundays, but invariably I was able to finish my class papers and projects more quickly because my Sundays of rest enabled me to work longer and more effectively the other six days of the week.

When we know the spiritual rest described in the previous chapter, we are thoroughly set free to rest physically. My Sabbath days often include sleeping later in the morning or taking naps or going to bed earlier at night. I try never to do anything that makes me feel unrestful. Once on a Sabbath afternoon I wrote to several friends and explained that I *should* have written to them the previous week and therefore did not. Because I felt I *had to* write those letters the previous week, it was very important that I postpone them and rest instead. The Sabbath is never a day to allow ourselves to be pushed (especially by our own false guilt or by others' expectations) into activity of any kind.

The emphasis upon physical rest as the meaning of the Sabbath is especially strong in the account of the commandment recorded in Deuteronomy 5:12-15. In contrast to the account in Exodus 20, which celebrates the Sabbath as an imitation of God's ceasing from his creative activity on the seventh day, the Deuteronomy passage says the following instead:

> Observe the Sabbath day by keeping it holy, as the LORD your God has commanded you. Six days you shall labor and do all your work, but the seventh day is a Sabbath to the LORD your God. On it you shall not do any work, neither you, nor your son or daughter, nor your manservant or

maidservant, nor your ox, your donkey or any of your animals, nor the alien within your gates, so that your manservant and maidservant may rest, as you do. Remember that you were slaves in Egypt and that the LORD your God brought you out of there with a mighty hand and an outstretched arm. Therefore the LORD your God has commanded you to observe the Sabbath day.

The commandment is quite clear: each person is to cease from work—not only the masters, but also all the servants and the foreigners and the animals. Give your donkey a break!

The motivation for letting the servants cease their working was that the Israelites had once had to work as slaves, and they knew how miserable that was. Therefore, in gratitude for Yahweh's delivering them out of their Egyptian bondage, they were to observe the Sabbath and allow everyone else not merely to quit working, too, but also genuinely to rest.

We might have trouble putting this idea into twentieth-century terms because, for many of us, our regular weekday work does not involve physical labor, whereas in biblical times most jobs involved great physical exertion. To the Israelites first receiving the command, it offered hope for a real reprieve from the arduous activity of trying to grow food in their hostile environment. As we cross the hermeneutical gap and seek to understand Sabbath rest in our times, we can look for a similar contrast between our weekday and Sabbath activity. If we are primarily engaged in physical exertion during the week, the Sabbath offers a physical respite. For those of us involved in the opposite rhythm of sedentary labor, the Sabbath offers a contrasting change of gentle physical enjoyment.

For me the Sabbath means several kinds of physical rest depending on what I do the week before and the week after each celebration. During most weeks I swim every day to take care of my health. Sunday offers a reprieve from that workout. I enter the water differently on Sundays—I enjoy just playing around in the pool or floating on the lake's waves. (What a nice break from doing laps!) For me to keep the Sabbath means to exercise in a way that concentrates on God or on other people. So I frequently enjoy hikes in the woods (which always lead to praising God for the beauty of his creation) or walks with friends (and then the focus is on positive and upbuilding interchanges).

I must also stress that we must often take extra care to make it possible to rest from our labors on the Sabbath. Sometimes it means doing extra work the day before or spreading our work out throughout the week a bit better so that the Sabbath can truly be restful. If I'm going to teach on Monday, I need to do the final review of my plans on Saturday—which usually means double duty, since I'm generally teaching on Sunday, too, and need to review those plans as well. But in the freedom I experience throughout the complete day of Sabbath rest I continually find that the extra effort to get everything done before Sunday is worth it.

Recently a schoolteacher asked me how teachers could rest on Sunday when they had to give report cards to their students on Monday. This question requires a threefold response. First of all, those who have seriously decided to practice Sabbath keeping will gradually learn how to restructure their work so that they can spread it out over the days preceding the Sabbath. Furthermore, the rest of the previous Sabbath will have released them to work more diligently during the week so that they will be better able to finish their work before the next Sabbath arrives. (Another schoolteacher friend of mine has discovered that to be the case.) Finally, let's not become legalistic! Sometimes in our fallible humanness we do not plan appropriately—and we wind up not able to finish everything that needs to be done by Monday. Then we have three choices: to stay up later on Saturday to finish, to get up earlier on Monday, or to use some of our Sabbath day. I personally so value having an entire day of rest and worship that I will gladly choose the first or second option rather than be forced by necessity (the opposite of grace indeed!) to spoil my day of ceasing and delight.

Interestingly, scientific research frequently offers confirming evidence for the value of God's principles as given in the

Scriptures. The interchange of physical activity and rest has been studied extensively by Juan-Cardos Lerman, whose research at the University of Arizona shows the biological need for rest every seventh day and the energizing value of rest.[1] According to Lerman's theory, failing to rest after six days of steady work will lead to insomnia or sleepiness, hormonal imbalances, fatigue, irritability, organ stress, and other increasingly serious physical and mental symptoms. Lerman suggests that this need for rest every seventh day is rooted in the fact that the human biological clock operates on a 25-hour cycle.[2] Because organized society prevents us from getting up one hour later each day to follow our natural internal clock, our body demands the time to "sleep in" or rest every so often to recover from the forced 24-hour time cycle that is too short. Lerman insists that we must "cease labor" once every seven days and rest our bodies for longer periods than on other days in order to catch up on our cycle of time. He also adds that the biblical Sabbath commandment includes the ideas of both cessation of labor and refreshment.

Of course, such scientific study doesn't "prove" the validity of God's command, since the purposes of science and faith are very different. But it is interesting that the methods of scientific inquiry have also led to the truth of God's design for rest, established long before in Sabbath commands.

An important warning immediately comes to mind as we pursue the subject of physical rest. It seems to me that our culture's obsession with audio and visual media has decreased the possibility of true physical rest. Our bodies are not able to rest when our senses are assaulted by advertisements and our sensibilities are bombarded with immoralities. There is a great

---

1. After Lerman addressed the American Association for the Advancement of Science in Tucson, Arizona, Carla McClain reported on his work in an article in *The Idaho Statesman* called "Human 'Clock' Orders Day Off."

2. This cycle was measured by monitoring changes in body temperature associated with times of sleep for people placed in constant light or constant darkness.

need in our society for the rest of silence. (See Chapter 22, which discusses the importance of silence in Sabbath keeping.)

One great tool for Sabbath resting in my childhood was the front porch swing. My family enjoyed sitting there and visiting with the neighbors who sauntered past. We talked gently and watched the fireflies. I wish there could be a resurgence of front porches in American architecture. To restore them could help rebuild a sense of neighborhood and community in our technologically cocooned world. If we had the possibility of resting on a porch swing, we might more easily learn again to watch fireflies and be friendly with our neighbors.

The world around us is beginning to recognize the need for better rest. A few years ago *U.S. News and World Report* featured an article called "Sabbaticals Spread from Campus to Business."[3] However, a clinical psychologist quoted in the article stated that many executives suffering from burnout returned to the same work after an extended leave and again exhibited the same burnout symptoms within sixty days.

Perhaps that is why a weekly cycle of work and physical rest had to be commanded by God rather than merely suggested. As Eugene Peterson, author of "The Pastor's Sabbath," insists, "Nothing less than a command has the power to intervene in the vicious, accelerating, self-perpetuating cycle of faithless and graceless busy-ness, the only part of which we are conscious being our good intentions." Peterson describes the Sabbath as that uncluttered time and space in which we can distance ourselves from our own activities enough to see what God is doing. If we are not able to rest one day a week, we are taking ourselves far too seriously.[4]

Since it is so hard to rest in our driven culture, a very essential contribution of the Christian community could be its sup-

---

3. "Sabbaticals Spread from Campus to Business," *U.S. News and World Report,* 25 Jan. 1985, pp. 79-80.
4. Peterson, "The Pastor's Sabbath," *Leadership,* Spring 1985, pp. 55-56.

port for those seeking to incorporate Sabbath rest into their life-styles. So many factors push us constantly, and we always have too much to do. Therefore, we as members of the Body of Christ need to help each other learn to rest. Ideally, we could covenant together to celebrate our Sabbaths in restful ways—taking gentle walks together, encouraging each other to sleep, helping each other know that the grace of God has set us free from the need to accomplish things.

We can also support one another in practical ways—for example, by sharing chores during the week so that they don't have to be done on Sundays. Sometimes I can do my friend Myron's laundry when I do my own, so that he can get other things done on Saturday (his only day off from teaching school) and thereby be freer to rest on the Sabbath. So many people are unable to practice the ideal of Sabbath ceasing from work—like musicians or cooks at a camp. I don't think it is work for us to give them the gift of assistance by setting up chairs or washing dishes with them. Every little bit of support that we can give each other is an important contribution to another's Sabbath rest.

Perhaps such support is implied in the Sabbath command in Deuteronomy 5. Perhaps the command for the masters to let their menservants and maidservants also rest is a reminder to the masters and mistresses themselves that they, too, are invited by Yahweh's instruction to give up their efforts and control and to enjoy the sweet repose of God's *menuha*.

10. Emotional Rest

ONE OF THE MOST HILARIOUS scenes in all of Scripture is the narrative of Elijah's encounter with the priests of Baal on the top of Mount Carmel. He challenged the priests to a duel of fire: Elijah would build an altar to Yahweh and the priests would build an altar to Baal, and each side would offer a bull and pray to see which god responded by sending fire to consume the sacrifice.

The scene is magnificently climactic. Elijah allows the priests of Baal to go first. They pray and cry, dance from morning till noon, and gash themselves, but nothing happens. They are at their wits' end because they get no response. Elijah taunts them, "Shout louder! . . . Maybe your god is busy or deep in thought or traveling. Or has your god gone to the bathroom?" (The Revised Standard Version translates that as "he has gone aside.") What kind of god do you have if he can't relieve himself and care about you at the same time?

This mockery is outrageously hilarious—and the whole encounter demonstrated very clearly that Baal was no god at all. Elijah's God, the covenant Yahweh, is, of course, the only true God. He manifested himself powerfully by sending fire down upon Elijah's altar, which had been drenched with twelve buckets of water both to symbolize the twelve tribes of Israel and to add to the tension, since water was a precious commodity after three years of drought. The scene is followed by the slaying of the false priests and the coming of the long-awaited rain. Certainly the day must have been incredibly emotional for Elijah. The challenge was exhausting (1 Kings 18:16-46).

Queen Jezebel, however, wasn't too thrilled with this turn of events. Those priests had served her god, Baal, and Elijah was a troublesome meddler. She immediately dispatched a messenger to inform Elijah that his fate would match that of her priests.

What would you do at this point if you were Elijah? I'm sure that I would run—just as he did. He hurried a day's journey into the desert and asked Yahweh to let him die. The life of a prophet was too tough.

The amazing thing is how Yahweh responded. He put Elijah to sleep!

Next God sent an angel to feed him, after which he took another nap. Then the angel came a second time to offer Elijah food to sustain him for the long trek to Horeb. There Yahweh appeared to Elijah, not in the customary form of wind, earthquake, or fire (images that immediately remind us of Mount Sinai and God's theophany there), but in a quiet, gentle whisper (1 Kings 19:1-12).

I have recounted this story at length because it speaks profoundly to an overwhelming need in our times—the need for emotional rest. So very often we are too emotionally drained to be able to cope with what is happening to us or because of us. The rush of time, the pace of change, the frenzy of demands upon us all leave us psychically exhausted.

In our lives we experience the same kinds of emotions that overwhelmed Elijah in the two days I've just described. No doubt he felt fear, exhilaration, terror, confidence, panic, delight, and doubt all mixed together. No wonder he wanted to die. Yet the first thing Yahweh does for him is put him to sleep.

This makes perfect sense. We cannot deal very well with

our emotional needs unless we are first physically rejuvenated. The Sabbath offers us physical rest—the ceasing of our labors and sleep to restore us—and then it offers us emotional rest, especially by giving us a new perspective.

I remember viewing a series of eight Impressionist paintings in a special exhibit and discovering that, when I stood in a new place, the painting that I liked least danced out of the corner with a new beauty. In the same way, the Sabbath gives us emotional rest by offering us a different place to stand in our relationship with God, with ourselves, and with the world.

After Elijah has been strengthened physically, God deals with his emotions by meeting him in a new way—in the quiet, gentle whisper of his tender love. God doesn't criticize Elijah for his doubts and fears, but meets him graciously, asks him why he is so upset, listens to his repeated complaint, and gives him new instructions for what to do next. All of these gifts offer Elijah space and tools for emotional healing. (They also give us precise models for how to minister to one another in our depressions.)

The Sabbath is a day set apart for deepening our relationship with God, and that necessarily leads to emotional healing. God meets us graciously in the reading of Scripture and the sermon, in the hymns and the liturgy, and in the prayers of our corporate worship services. He reveals himself to us in tender and compassionate ways. Moreover, God meets us in our personal prayers, which give us the opportunity to pour out our feelings— knowing that God will listen. In our quiet devotional times, too, God often gives us specific instructions for proceeding with whatever is happening in our lives. A special day set aside for prayer and meditation is a great gift for our emotional healing.

Because our technological society fosters a blasé lack of commitment, our emotions often suffer as the result of our lack of commitment to our own true selves. A day set apart for emotional rest gives us the silence to discover ourselves, to recover our integrity and creativity (as we shall see more deeply in several chapters later in this book).

Also, as we deepen our relationships with others—another

integral part of our Sabbath celebrations—those individuals bring us gifts of emotional rest, too. I remember how freeing Sabbaths were for me during my years in Indiana because often my friend Diana and I would have supper and go to a concert together. During those times she enabled me to unload a lot of emotional baggage that was weighing me down. The music, too, brought great healing. (Now that I live elsewhere, I really miss all the concerts and recitals of the university environment.) Beautiful music always lifts my emotional life to God and fills me with an awed sense of his majesty and creativity. Sometimes Diana herself, a pianist, was giving or participating in the concert. On those occasions she offered her great musical gifts as her own Sabbath worship and to deepen the worship of others—especially mine, as I heard God's grace through the artistry of my dear friend.

A great part of the emotional healing of the Sabbath lies in its contribution of both solitude and community. We need silent spaces, times for reflection and meditation. On the other hand, we also need communal interaction, and the activities of the Sabbath day encourage family unity, leisurely conversation, and growing friendships. Through our Sabbath keeping we can learn to rest both in our own personalities and in our relationships.

Furthermore, solitude and community work together in paradox. Our times of solitude make our times of community deeper because we have learned more about ourselves to offer to the whole. Reciprocally, our times in community rebuild our sense of self through interaction with others and give us food for our personal reflections. Thus, the rhythm of Sabbath times alone and together with others can bring great healing rest to our emotional lives.

In our modern world emotional strains often continue to build in our lives because so many things lie outside of our power and understanding. That is why hobbies are so helpful—because they give us a little piece of life over which we can have control. We can feel good about ourselves when we successfully sew a new outfit or crochet a present for a friend, when we build a model train car, when we can name the birds that come to our feeder.

As an alternative to the world's methods, Sabbath spirituality offers us several means to combat the "out-of-control-ness" of modern society. First of all, its very order and rhythm bring about emotional rest. When so much of life is unsure and dependent upon circumstances beyond our control, the sureness of one day in every seven to set everything aside gives us emotional stability.

Moreover, on the Sabbath day we deliberately remember that we have ceased trying to be God and instead have put our lives back into his control. Concentrating on God's Lordship in our lives enables us to return to his sovereign hands all the things that are beyond our control and terrifying us. Once those things are safely there, and as long as we don't stupidly take them back again, our emotions can find truly comforting and healing rest.

A particular case in point concerns the needs of a single person for emotional nurture. Sometimes I struggle with great fear that in the future my needs for personal support will not be met. The spiritual rest of the Sabbath continually reminds me that God's grace undergirds my life, and that he cares intimately—as demonstrated in the case of Elijah—for my emotional well-being. Our times of worship and of sharing with others in the fellowship of the Christian community enfold us so that we can rest in the belief that God's provision for all our needs will always also include the emotional as well as the physical and spiritual.

We can also find great rest in realizing that our emotions are not the foremost determiner of our lives. Our culture tells us, "If it feels good, do it," or that we have to obey our emotions when we are tempted. Sabbath keeping reminds us that our wills are stronger than our emotions, that we can resist the temptations that our emotions put to us, that we can even deliberately change our emotions by an act of will. Do not get me wrong: I'm not advocating that we repress our emotions—which can lead to great scarring. Instead I'm advocating that we put emotions back into their proper place as the caboose of our train of living. Our will or deliberate thinking is the engine, and our emotions properly just come along for the ride.

We must pay attention to our emotions, of course; I'm certainly not urging us to become emotionally sterile robots without any feelings whatsoever. Rather, letting God be God in our lives gives us the freedom to deal constructively with our emotions, to accept them and listen to them, but not to be controlled by them. In fact, ceasing our striving to be God lets us rest in our true emotions and appreciate all the nuances of our own personalities.

As we well know, the pressures of life put us out of touch with our deepest feelings and inner desires. A day of Sabbath rest satisfies our profound need for time to allow ourselves to feel, to be sensitive, to experience all the gifts of life more thoroughly. We discover all the emotions that have been buried in the rush of work, and then we can appreciate those deepest feelings that are the genuine components of our personhood.

One of the delights of my new home is that several of my neighbors have lovely rosebushes, and in this warm fall during which I am beginning to write this book, the roses have lasted long past their usual tenure. Every day as I walk to my mailbox at the other end of the apartment row, I delight in the fragrances of the different kinds of roses that are still blooming gloriously. This experience is much like the keeping of the Sabbath. Even as my mail walk in the midst of my working day gives me a chance to enjoy my sensitivity to fragrances, so the Sabbath rest in between days of work gives us the chance to enjoy all the emotions that otherwise might lie hidden. We can stop to smell the roses, jump into leaves with ecstasy, appreciate the colors and songs and textures of our world, cry from the depths of our souls, laugh from the inmost recesses of our spirits, shout for Joy because our God is good.

These descriptions take us into the realm of the embracing and feasting that we will discuss more thoroughly in the final two sections of this book. Instead of pursuing them further at this point, we will turn now to another kind of rest that we can experience when we keep the Sabbath.

11. Intellectual Rest

L ET ME ALONE. I need some time to think."
One of the stultifying effects of our culture is that it
doesn't give us much time for creative and reflective thinking. We need all of our thinking time just to keep in touch with
what is going on, to cope with what is happening to us, in us,
and because of us. However, the fragmented nature of our experience prevents us from grasping a coherent view of the whole.

One of the best analyses of all of this is Jacques Ellul's
Humiliation of the Word, which laments the fact that our view of
reality is so distorted by the "news," which comes to us in small,
disjointed pieces that change every day and that usually focus on
the catastrophic. The result is that we develop an inadequate
perspective on world events and a consequent dwindling of our
sense of hope and meaning. We don't have much time to think
about any of the headlines except when they impinge on us
directly, and then our view is usually an isolated one that does
not take into consideration the relationship of that one dimension to the whole of our situation.

Sabbath keeping offers us the time to gain a larger perspective, to view our fragmented existence in light of a larger whole—

in Jacques Ellul's terms, to view our visible reality in light of the invisible, and larger, Truth.[1] The visible reality of our world, for example, includes numerous wars, political messes, economic chaos, and disrupted weather patterns, but the Truth that nevertheless prevails and gives us hope is that our gracious God is still sovereign over the universe and ultimately bringing his purposes to completion. This broader perspective re-establishes our bearings. Our concentration on who God is, as part of our Sabbath keeping, gives us a new framework in which to refocus our thinking in the days to come.

Related to this is the fact that Sabbath keeping enables us to understand the larger purposes of God and to place our intellectual work within that cosmic framework. Our culture fosters a specialization that leads many scholars to confine their efforts to minor matters. When by faith we take our position in the heavenly places (Eph. 2:6), we can become detached enough from the world's notions of success to understand more clearly what God intends to do in the world and thereby to find more carefully our place within his purposes. By making this point I am not rejecting specialization in itself when it is properly tempered by an overview of the whole. What I object to is the frenzy of the world's activity, the strain for prominence and success, the empty intellectualizing that serves only to elevate the thinker and not to contribute to the well-being of others in the world. Instead, our intellectual pursuits could solve problems or help others think or stir faith.

In the silence of our Sabbath observation our minds can rest, and that often leads to the freedom to learn anew how best to use our minds for the glory of God. To cease our laboring and rest our brains dispels the frenzied fear that drives our minds when we fall prey to the world's expectations for accomplishment. In addition, our intellectual rest gives us the courage to give up any senseless thinking or intellectual pride that might thwart God's purposes.

---

1. Ellul, *The Humiliation of the Word*, trans. Joyce Main Hanks (Grand Rapids: William B. Eerdmans, 1985), pp. 10-11.

Moreover, since to keep the Sabbath means to rest thoroughly, on that day we can rest from our usual kinds of intellectual labors. We don't have to think about the things that occupy our minds during our workdays. Such a temporary setting aside of those problems refreshes us so that we can return to our usual subjects of thought with new eagerness.

I noticed this particularly one Sunday during the time I was revising this book. After spending many previous weekends out of town for speaking engagements, I finally had a Sabbath at home. I enjoyed immensely the opportunities to worship in my home congregation, serve a special lunch to a good friend, take a nap, pick roses for every room of my apartment, take a walk in the fall breeze to visit some friends, and pray for four other friends as I wrote them letters. The next day I returned to the task of revising with new enthusiasm.

Sabbath keeping also directly affects our attitudes. When we are rested, we can think more objectively. Oftentimes our great frustrations in thinking arise because our perspectives are so clouded by the immediate impact of problems or pressures or pains. After setting everything aside for a day and ceasing to stew about it during our Sabbath celebration, we can think more clearly.

Furthermore, the delight we experience in keeping the Sabbath frees us to be more realistic. We can face the negative dimensions of the world and of our more immediate worlds with a realism born out of our knowledge that God is still Lord over everything that seems so crazy, that the invisible Truth of his love is larger than the visible reality of this world's pain.

Holy time also creates calm. Not only will that calmness last into the rest of the week and enable us to think things through more thoroughly, but also it will free us to be more creative. Some of my best thoughts are generated in the stillness of Sabbath keeping, and I frequently experience sudden moments of more complete understanding because resting my mind renews it and because I can think more organically when my thinking isn't forced. I try to let creativity roam freely as long as it will and then jot down the new discoveries in my journal for further reflection.

However, I also think it is important not to *work at* thinking on the Sabbath day. Whenever our creativity begins to be onerous, it destroys our Sabbath resting.

That is why it is so critical for me to be very strict with myself about not working on the Sabbath. I try not to think about whatever writing project I have in the works or about upcoming Bible studies to prepare. If new thoughts come to me, I consider them special Sabbath gifts from God and receive them gladly, but I try not to let myself *work* on them.

Perhaps my teaching of Sunday-morning Bible classes provides a good illustration. People who have heard me talk about Sabbath keeping often ask me, "But what about preachers who have to give sermons or organists and choir directors who are responsible for music in our worship services? We can't get along without them. And what about you—you're teaching this class on the Sabbath." That is true, but for me teaching a class is utter delight and usually the setting for a new experience of the Holy Spirit's empowering. (I feel the same way whenever I play the organ, direct or sing in a choir, or give a sermon on a Sunday morning.) However, I do not do any studying or practicing for those tasks on Sabbath morning! All my studying must be done in the days or weeks beforehand. Then, when it is time for me to teach, the Spirit can bring to my mind what I have learned and also give me new insights as I speak. That freedom to listen to the Spirit isn't possible if I haven't done my homework—the language study, the outlining, and the meditating that go into preparing a class. Yet the Sabbath is a day for intellectual rest, so I want to be sure that I have done all my homework before I lie down to sleep on Saturday night.

Then what fun the Sabbath is! I can enjoy to the hilt the creativity made possible by the intellectual rest of the day and experience the closeness to God that always overwhelms me when I have the privilege of handling the beautiful texts of the Scriptures. What a thrill it is to meet God in his Word! I feel so grateful that he graciously lets me be his servant to lead others into the biblical discoveries that he has prepared for us.

Obviously, it can't always be such "sweetness and light." All kinds of things go wrong. All sorts of hindrances block our Sabbath freedom. Yet the meaning of the Sabbath as a ceasing and a resting day frees us from being too hassled by such things. We can learn good lessons from the troubles we encounter and seek to prevent them in the future by making better preparations in the days before the Sabbath. Remember that the descriptions in this book are ideals. Certainly we will not be able to celebrate the Sabbath perfectly, but we don't have to let the discrepancies between our visions and our imperfect realization of them spoil the benefits of our Sabbath keeping. Each week provides a new opportunity to enjoy the Sabbath as thoroughly as we can.

One of the reasons that the intellectual rest of Sabbath keeping is so important stems from the fact that the Holy Spirit works primarily through the renewal of our minds—as the Scriptures continually remind us. The following exhortation from Paul's letter to the Romans is especially descriptive:

> Therefore, I urge you, brothers and sisters, with eyes wide open to the mercies of God, as an act of intelligent worship, to offer your bodies as living sacrifices, holy and pleasing to God. Do not conform any longer to the pattern of this world, but be transformed by the renewing of your mind, so that you may prove in practice that the plan of God for you is good, acceptable, and moves toward the goal of true maturity.[2]

Intelligent worship is the way to avoid the pressures of the world around us to conform to its values and goals. When our eyes are opened to the richness of God's mercies (in spiritual rest), we can offer our bodies to God as living sacrifices—which means that we can die to all our own efforts to be holy and pleasing to God by letting him consume us with the holy fire of his grace. As J. B. Phillips phrases it, we don't have to let the world

---

2. Rom. 12:1-2 in a composite of the NIV and J. B. Phillips' *New Testament in Modern English*.

around us squeeze us into its mold. Instead, we can be remolded from the inside—and God's means for doing that is the renewing of our minds. The Greek word *anakainosis,* which we translate "renewing," suggests a major renovation in our thinking.

When a building is renovated, old materials are removed so that the new can be constructed more sturdily with better materials. In the same way, we need Sabbath resting from our old intellectual patterns in order to bring in the new building blocks of the spiritual perspectives with which God wants to order our thinking. We need such an intellectual overhaul weekly—otherwise we get more and more entrapped in the thinking patterns of the world. Too easily we can fall into its cynicism and despair, its overly objective rationality and technological sterility, instead of building our thinking with materials of true realism and hope, a balanced subjectivity and objectivity, the warmth of God's compassionate wisdom.

Sabbath keeping gives us time to rest from the struggle of thinking as Christians in a post-Christian world. It lets us focus our thoughts upon God without distraction. Into this holy time the Spirit comes with renewing power and transforms our thinking from the inside into new patterns in line with the perfect wisdom of God.

12. Aids to Rest

SEVERAL OF MY OWN Sabbath practices have already been mentioned in this book. Now it is time to pause awhile to consider what practices you might want to develop in order to let your Sabbath keeping be a holy time of ceasing and laying aside work, productivity, worry, striving to be God, possessing, and all the other entrapments of our culture and its meaninglessness. What gifts in your life enable you to rest? It will help if we think of aids to each of the kinds of rest we have already discussed in this section.

In the first place, what sorts of practices or objects might help you to rest more completely in God's grace? What is conducive to your having a deeper experience of God's presence in a special way? An effective tool that brings me into God's presence is beauty—in many different forms and stimulating all the senses. Lovely music, the majesty of nature in mountains and flowers and fall leaves and winter snows, the fragrance of candles and spices, the softness and warmth of afghans, the taste of communion bread and wine, the embrace of children and close friends, the mystery of works of art—all these things lead me to experience the presence of the Creator-Designer.

Perhaps those are not things that enable you to experience the gentle whisper of God. I offer my lists only to nudge your own reflection. As you consider what kinds of things bring you to true rest, you will be naming things that are conducive to ushering you into God's presence.

I also experience spiritual rest through whatever inspires my creativity in praising God. Playing various musical instruments, for example, is a way for me to praise God. (I have a piano, a guitar, a Celtic harp, three recorders, an African kalimba, a Japanese xylophone, and lots of rhythm instruments!) I love jam sessions, because nobody really cares how good she or he is. We can all be free to make joyful noises to the Lord without needing to accomplish anything worth concertizing.

Most of all, meditation on God's Word brings us to spiritual rest. I especially enjoy reading not technical works on the Scriptures (which is frequently part of my weekday work), but works that focus on praising God—C. S. Lewis's Narnia Chronicles, the novels of George MacDonald, hymns, poems, inspirational books filled with beautiful pictures, mystical works, books that simply rejoice in the truth of God's Word. Spending extra time just thinking about Bible texts is a privilege I'm not usually afforded in the rush of busy weekdays.

Of course, all the kinds of rest in our Sabbath keeping interlock. Whatever gives us physical rest will probably also put us more deeply in touch with the grace of God. Moreover, when we are physically rested, we will be more at rest emotionally, too. What is important to remember here is that certain activities and objects are especially conducive to the various kinds of Sabbath rest.

In thinking about physical rest we might consider, first of all, what sorts of traditions help us slow our pace. When I was a child, my family slowed its pace every Sunday evening with the custom of inviting over for supper some of the faculty members from the Lutheran school of which my father was principal and in which my mother taught. The menu every week was the same: hotdogs by the fireplace. That is certainly not a gourmet meal, but those evenings were so special to me that I recently invited three of my godchildren and their parents over for a Sunday evening of hotdogs and music-making. The custom offered a great change of pace for my parents, who usually were extremely busy with all the work of running a school and teaching in it. The warm atmosphere of friends around a cozy fireplace seemed to slow them down and give them time to relax.

The fireplace in my apartment does the same thing for me. To sit by it invites gazing into the glowing coals. The gladsome crackling of the logs welcomes frequent glancing up from whatever I'm reading. The fire's cozy warmth enhances gentle conversation with my guests.

Having company (with or without a fire) also slows my pace. It pulls me away from any thoughts of work into the grace of relaxation. That is why one of my favorite things to do on a Sabbath day is to invite special people over for a dinner party. Let me emphasize that I keep the cooking simple; it would spoil the whole value of Sabbath rest to go to all sorts of elaborate trouble to create an exotic menu. I trust that the dinner can be made beautiful by caring touches such as using china and candles and making things as lovely as I can, and especially by not being hassled myself in any efforts to impress anybody.

Previously I mentioned changing activities in order to enjoy the physical rest of the Sabbath—not pushing hard in the swimming pool if that is how we work out during the week, or choosing to go for an easy walk instead. A bicycle is an excellent aid to rest, as is a rocking chair or a warm bed!

Emotional rest is especially induced by whatever calls forth our creativity and spontaneity. Last year on the first Sabbath afternoon in February I had a great time making valentines. Having had no opportunity to get to a store, I lacked the usual materials for making fancy, decorated ones. What fun it was to find a way to express my love to those dearest to me without the usual paraphernalia. (I finally found a way to use some leftover pieces of old cardboard to invite my loved ones to realize that without their support my days of graduate work would have been similarly stiff and gray!) This activity gave me emotional rest not only because it created an opportunity for me to give affection, but also because it let me discover new creativity in myself.

Paradoxically, both solitude and company are conducive to emotional rest for me. Sometimes a walk alone (in the presence of God) brings vast emotional healing, but at other times pouring out my sadnesses to a friend is more helpful. For each of us, those things that will give us emotional rest either take us away from the emotions that unsettle us or give us enough emotional security to face whatever afflicts us.

Similarly, the things most conducive to intellectual rest are those aids that either lead us into new, creative paths of thinking or strengthen our minds in God so that the painful thinking that we have to do in days to come is undergirded. My favorite way to receive God's gift of intellectual rest is through reading stories and fairy tales. During the eight weeks preceding my comprehensive exams I read a George MacDonald story every Sunday. I love the goodness of his main characters, their virtuous behavior; they always inspire me to choose God's ways and create in me a great yearning to be more loving and good. Especially on the day before the exams began, I found it immensely refreshing to set all the months of preparing aside, to cease that intellectual work altogether, and to enjoy instead the intellectual rest of a good story. Good fairy tales also give great emotional healing because they turn out well; they create in us new hope and trust.

The best aid to all the forms of Sabbath rest is God's gift of holy time. In our workweek we don't have adequate time for everything. We cannot set our work aside; we can't afford the interruption of letting our emotional reserve down; we must focus our intellect on the tasks at hand. The result is that we easily lose sight of God's grace underneath everything. Consequently, when our Sabbath keeping puts us more firmly in touch again with the comprehensiveness of God's grace, it enables us to experience rest in all its fullness. That is why it is so important to observe a whole day of Sabbath—an entire twenty-four hours of pure Sabbath keeping. That gives us plenty of time to cease our labors and experience true rest.

13. Social Rest

IHAVE NEVER HEARD the phrase "social rest." Instead, we usually hear a lot about *social unrest.* An exciting aspect of Sabbath keeping is the fact that it leads to very practical consequences both in our immediate communities and in our confused, war-torn world.

Both the intensity of my commitment to Sabbath keeping and the fervency of my desire to care about the hungry and to build peace in the world have been growing side by side over the last several years. Only recently did I begin to realize that all these things are tied quite closely together.

The first major shattering of the complacent world of my childhood came between my junior and senior years of college. I had run into some very tough health problems before that, but those personal problems were enfolded in the larger world, which still seemed to be primarily safe and good. I grew up in the midst of prosperous tomato country in Ohio and lived quite a sheltered life among strong Christians.

When I participated in a college-choir tour around the world, however, my eyes were suddenly opened to the immense problem of world hunger. During the ten days that we performed concerts in India to strengthen the Lutheran Church there, we saw thousands of beggars, hundreds of bodies lying in the streets, and scores of large wheelbarrows into which the dead were scooped to be carted to the city dump to be burned. Everything turned upside down for me there; my whole understanding of the world was changed. I knew that I had to spend the rest of my life campaigning and fighting against world hunger and poverty.

After I finished college and was working as a Bible teacher, I became more and more troubled by the constant challenge from Jesus to love our enemies. Since he also commanded us to feed them, my concern for peace became connected to my previously awakened economic concerns. Then, when I began to learn how the militarization of the world is the leading reason for the lack of resources to feed the poor, my growing desires to be working for peace and against hunger became thoroughly conjoined.

Meanwhile, I had also begun to feel that something was out of whack in the church. Why did we pay attention to the commands not to steal and not to kill, but, in far too many cases, did not pay attention to the commands to observe the Sabbath day and to refrain from adultery? The more I thought about that question, the more I realized that we have never really paid attention to any of the commandments, beginning with our refusal to honor Yahweh, our God, and to serve him only. We may not steal by robbing a bank or kill by murdering our spouses, but Christians are involved in the stealing from the poor that present economic policies foster, as well as in the killing that is done in the name of "preserving democracy."

Thus, these biblical concerns came together, and I saw that they are all of a piece. Our refusals to worship only Yahweh and to worship him especially on a day set apart for that purpose are inextricably intertwined with our refusal to love the poor, the hungry, and the enemy. All of our refusals reject the wisdom of God's instructions for our lives. We think we know better than God how to make ourselves happy, so we ignore all these instructions he gave us for truly enjoying life: to be devoted to the One who creates life; to live in a rhythm of six days of work and one day of Sabbath ceasing, resting, embracing, and feasting; to live out our sexuality in healthy relationships according to God's design; and to love our neighbors and our enemies by seeking to build both economic stability and political peace.

On the positive side, if we devote a special day to the worship of God, we will be changed so much by that Sabbath keeping—spiritually, physically, emotionally, intellectually, and socially—that our service to God and to others will fall more in line with the rest of the commandments. To choose to keep the Sabbath will irrevocably transform how we relate to the rest of the world. I am using the term "social rest" to name the subject of this chapter because the easing of anxieties, the shifting of attitudes away from our American intensity about accomplishment and productivity, the emotional rest and all the other factors that we have been discussing in our sections on ceasing and resting will enable us to behave differently in the midst of the world's tensions. I am utterly convinced that if all the Christians in the world could thoroughly practice Sabbath keeping, we could also learn that we don't need to kill each other.

A poster on the living-room wall of my apartment in Indiana depicted a black person and a white person embracing each other and issued this critical challenge: "A Modest Proposal for Peace: Let All the Christians of the World Decide That They Will Not Kill Each Other." Imagine what could happen in the world if we Christians took that seriously!

The peace-building inherent in Sabbath keeping goes back to our Jewish roots. In *My Mother's Sabbath Days*, Chaim Grade recounts several incidents in which his mother explicitly curbed her tongue in order not to desecrate the Sabbath. When Chaim was a child, one of his neighbors rebuked him with the words, "Whoever heard of a Jewish boy having such goyish violence in him?"[1]

---

1. Grade, *My Mother's Sabbath Days: A Memoir*, trans. Channa Kleinerman Goldstein and Inna Hecker Grade (New York: Alfred A. Knopf, 1986), p. 12. The term *goyish* refers to the Gentiles, whose violence is not in keeping with the character of those who observe the Sabbath.

The Mishnah,[2] compiled around 200 C.E., teaches that the Sabbath law against the carrying of any kind of burden in the public domain includes weapons, that "man should not walk out with sword, bow and arrow, shield, spear or lance" on the holy day. In later discussion as recorded in the Talmud, Rabbi Eliezer disagreed on the grounds that the weapons were ornaments attached to the body, which one might carry on Shabbat. The majority of rabbis decided otherwise, however, and retorted to Rabbi Eliezer,

> Those weapons are nothing but a shame to man, for did not Isaiah prophesy that the time would come that "the nations shall beat their swords into plowshares and their spears into pruning hooks; nation shall not lift up sword against nation, neither shall they learn war any more." If that is the ultimate ideal of universal history, how may weapons have any ornamental significance![3]

In the Middle Ages the hierarchy of the Church was able to convince the Christians of the Western world not to kill each other on the Sabbath day (celebrated on Sunday) and other festival days. Since most of the groups fighting each other were at least politically Christian, the priests were able to enforce what was called "the Truce of God." On those days there would be no fighting so that the warring peoples could worship. By extending the days that were observed under the aegis of "the Truce of God," the priests were able to reduce greatly the amount of conflict. Even during the World Wars, Christian peasants sometimes served Christmas dinners to isolated enemy soldiers.

What wonderful timing that while I was writing this chapter I received a telephone call from a good friend of mine who

---

2. The Mishnah is the earliest compilation of rabbinic reflection on the Torah. The Talmud includes the Mishnah and the Gemara, which is a commentary on the Mishnah. For a more complete list of the earliest rabbinic works, see footnote 4 in Chapter 15.

3. Eliezer Berkovitz, *Not in Heaven: The Nature and Function of Halakha* (New York: Ktav, 1983), p. 20.

spends much of his life working for peace. When I mentioned this idea of "the Truce of God," Glen said it sounded just like the recent "Great American Smokeout," in which many smokers all tried to quit on the same day. The intention was that their success and enjoyment of the smoke-free experience would inspire them to quit smoking entirely. Perhaps in the same way, if Christians all decided not to kill each other on the Sabbath Day, they would soon extend that to the other days of the week and cease the practice altogether.

What might be the implications of such a Truce of God in a nuclear age? In our post-Christian world, of course, we can no longer impose such an idea on entire nations in conflict. But what could it mean in its practical application if all Christians were convinced that we ought not to kill each other?

To keep the Sabbath causes us to rethink more seriously the command of Jesus to love our enemies. To cease our productivity and need to accomplish also lessens our need to be better than the next guy. To rest—especially to rest emotionally—reduces hostilities.

These effects of Sabbath keeping pertain to hostilities on all levels. During the last several years I have found that true Sabbath keeping forces me to reconsider all my relationships in which hostilities are occurring—relationships with immediate family and friends, with neighbors and people in my Christian community, as well as in the global community. I say "true Sabbath keeping" because I can always ignore God's nudging if I want to—and that would be far easier—rather than face the fact that the hostilities are largely due to my pride or my spiteful behavior or my distorted sense of things. Sabbath keeping fosters instead an increase in our gentleness and tenderness, a non-aggressive stance toward others, the ability to dismantle our own power.

On the interpersonal level, keeping the Sabbath is a good way to be held accountable to God for our relationships. I can't enjoy a day set apart for fellowship with him if my relationships with others whom he has also created are out of whack. To receive his grace and to experience his restoration of my broken and sinful life stirs me to want restoration for everyone. To discover ourselves enfolded by grace in the holiness of God causes us to desire that same celebration for each person.

Furthermore, Sabbath keeping exposes our political illusions. To think about God and the lifestyle to which he calls us forces us to see that our political power plays do not accomplish God's purposes. Just as the Israelites needed to heed Isaiah's warning that their efforts to secure military alliances and to trust in weapons were futile, so we need to recognize the truth of Yahweh's warning that "in repentance and rest is your salvation; in quietness and trust is your strength" (Isa. 30:15). Instead of scrambling for security in national victory and domination, in preparations for war and military aggression, we must relearn the values of cooperation and sharing, of nonviolence and support.

We live in such a harsh society. The technology that brings us all kinds of benefits also brings impersonalization, a loss of control over our own circumstances, and radiation-caused cancer. Frenzy about time, possessions, sex, and status leads to violence, rage, rape, technological aggression, exploitation, and manipulation. The humility and serenity engendered by Sabbath keeping empower us to be agents of healing both near and far. Our prayers at Sabbath dinner might include the petition that our own privilege of celebrating would remind us of the needs of others and deepen our activity in caring for the hungry. Similarly, the prayers for Sabbath peace in our own lives will inevitably lead us to prayers and action for the peace of the world.

In the passage from *The Sabbath* quoted in Chapter 8, Abraham Heschel uses the word *harmony* to define *menuha*, or Sabbath rest. For Jews *menuha* included harmony with all others, the absence of strife, fighting, fear, and distrust. In the same way, the New Testament letter to the Ephesians exclaims that Christ has broken down the barriers that sin has created between people. No longer do Jews and Gentiles have to be divided, for Christ has given them both access to the Father through the Spirit so that the Gentiles can be "fellow citizens with God's people and members of God's household" (Eph. 2:14-19). Hostility between ethnic groups in the Church has been ended, so the opposing sides can learn to love one another. Furthermore, together they can be agents for racial reconciliation and economic redistribution and tension reduction in the world.

Most of this chapter has concentrated on the peace-building dimension of social rest because the Church has so often been an agent of war instead of reconciliation. We must specifically note, however, that perhaps the most effective way to seek peace in the world is by working for justice. We will discuss the feeding of the hungry more thoroughly in Chapter 25, but here we must remember that the biblical concept of the Sabbath also includes precepts concerning the Sabbath years and the Jubilee, precepts about justice. Every seven years the land was to be allowed to rest; every "seven sabbaths of years" (Lev. 25:8) property was to be returned to its original owners (Lev. 25:28). By such equalization, economic balance was to be maintained and the Jews would be able to "live safely in the land" (Lev. 25:18).

Perhaps if God's people again observed the Sabbath, we would become more of a Jubilee people—setting free those oppressed by economic injustice, canceling debts, restoring the land, and thereby building peace. My prayer has been that this book will reawaken a desire among Christians to keep the Sabbath. That prayer is extended by the petition that our Sabbath keeping in the Church will also issue in justice keeping and peace keeping in the world.

14. An Ethics of Character

IN THE FINAL CHAPTER of the previous section on ceasing we saw in a more comprehensive way that all the dimensions of Sabbath ceasing free us from the humdrum and the meaninglessness of the culture which surrounds us. Similarly, in this chapter we recognize that all the aspects of resting which we have discussed in this section lead to a more comprehensive understanding of the nature of Christian ethics.

First of all, our ethics are founded upon the grace of God, as accentuated in the chapter on spiritual rest. We do not make moral choices because we *have to* live in a certain way; we don't discipline ourselves to behave in certain ways because we have to carve out our lifestyle by our own efforts. Ours is an ethic of freedom,[1] of loving response because God loved us first.

Second, the value of our work is determined by our Sabbath rest (in contrast to our society's ethics, in which work deter-

---

1. My thanks to Jacques Ellul, who taught me this fundamental description of Christian ethics in his major work, *The Ethics of Freedom*, trans. and ed. Geoffrey W. Bromiley (Grand Rapids: William B. Eerdmans, 1976).

mines the value of everything else) — a point emphasized in the chapter on physical rest. This leads to valuing persons not for their accomplishments, but for who they are. We discover new serenity in our lives when we allow ourselves to *be* rather than forcing ourselves to *do.*

Furthermore, the emotional and intellectual rest of the Sabbath day keeps us from blocking God as the Spirit works to transform our minds and personalities from the inside. He sets us free and empowers us to become more fully the people he has designed us to be. Moreover, this is true on a worldwide scale, as seen in the previous chapter, which connects Sabbath keeping with peace-building. If we become people of peace through the intentionality of our Sabbath keeping, then we will, out of that character of peacemaking, live in a way that promotes peace.

All of this means that the Sabbath rhythm leads to an ethics of *becoming* (how our character is being developed) and not of *doing* (how we react in specific situations). By the latter I refer to ethical systems that concentrate on making moral decisions in particular circumstances on the basis of what rules to follow or what results will be gained by a certain action. An ethics of character concentrates instead on what kind of people we are becoming. If the Holy Spirit has developed certain virtues in us, then in any particular case our behavior will issue from that character.

Nicholas Wolterstorff emphasizes that the very practice of weekly worship and rest is an essential part of the character of the Christian. In his book entitled *Until Justice and Peace Embrace,* he asserts that "a rhythmic alternation of work and worship, labor and liturgy is one of the significant distinguishing features of the Christian's way of being-in-the-world." Furthermore, as this chapter has stressed and as Section IV will develop, Sabbath rest is not the rest of exhaustion or an escape from boredom, but a rest of delight, even as God delighted in his creation when he rested on the seventh day.[2]

---

2. Wolterstorff, *Until Justice and Peace Embrace* (Grand Rapids: William B. Eerdmans, 1983), pp. 147 and 153.

Sabbath keeping changes our character. We will be irrevocably transformed by the commitment to a special day set aside for our relationship with God, and that transformation will result in thinking and attitudes and emotions and behavior consistent with the character of the God who is the focus of our Sabbath keeping.

The reverse is also true. Since the Hebrew Scriptures and the Scriptures of the early Church (i.e., the Old and New Testaments) reveal God's intentions for the character of the Christian community, our growth as members of that Body will call us to a new faithfulness to God's revelation, which includes the injunction to observe the Sabbath day and keep it holy. The more we worship Yahweh, our God, and desire to serve him only, the more we will want to be like him and to follow his instructions against idolatry, killing, stealing, adultery, and coveting, and his commands to honor parents and keep the Sabbath.

Resting provides the necessary time for the Spirit's molding of our characters. The next section of this book, which concentrates on embracing, will focus on the values that God enables us to choose and practice in our Sabbath keeping so that we can become the people he has designed us to be. The more intentional we are about our choices, the more God's Spirit can work in us to develop a certain character, a certain set of virtues, a lifestyle of godliness.

This is not to be an onerous burden for us—that is why the last section of this book focuses on the feasting, the celebrating, that living the values of Sabbath keeping entails. Fundamental to it all, certainly, is the true resting in God's grace that sets us free. We can't find that rest, however, unless we have ceased to buy into the values of the culture around us. Thus, all the sections of this book are closely intertwined. All that we will discuss about embracing and feasting in the next two sections is built upon the ceasing and resting we have already celebrated.

PART III
EMBRACING

*All who keep the Sabbath without desecrating it
and who hold fast to my covenant—
these I will bring to my holy mountain
and give them joy in my house of prayer.*

—Isaiah 56:6-7

*The important point in all our imitation [of God] is its
deliberate intentionality. We don't just think God's values
are good. We embrace them wholly. . . . To embrace is to
accept with gusto, to live to the hilt, to choose with extra
intentionality and tenacity.*

—Marva Dawn

SABBATH KEEPING is not just negative ceasing. In the previous section we saw that all the Sabbath forms of resting correlate positively with our ceasing the productivity, worry, and striving that negatively character-ize our society. Even more positive is the subject of this section, our embracing of Sabbath values. We will begin with the intentionality and deliberateness that characterize the lifestyle of those who keep the Sabbath. Then we will consider how important it is that we as a Sabbath people deliberately embrace the values of the Christian communi-ty. In making this choice we embrace time instead of space and giving instead of requiring. In response to the grace of God we gladly embrace our calling in life, and in the full-ness of healing brought by our relationship with God we can embrace the wholeness of God's *shalom*. Finally, all these Sabbath gifts set us free to embrace the world.

As you can see, these elements of embracing God's kingdom and his purposes move us beyond the repentance of ceasing and the faith of resting into the application of the Christian lifestyle. By embracing God's instructions in response to his immense grace and love, we choose to im-itate God. This notion of imitation is rooted in Exodus 20:10-11, which emphasizes that when we abstain from work on the Sabbath we imitate Yahweh, who rested on the seventh day and therefore made it holy. The idea that the Israelites were holy because they belonged to God and that they therefore incorporated Yahweh's qualities into their lives by conscious imitation has been a very strong component of the Judaic concept of time and Sabbath throughout their history.[1] Many folktales even tell how the

---

1. Diana R. Engel, *The Hebrew Concept of Time and the Effect on the Development of the Sabbath* (Washington, D.C.: American University Press, 1976).

Sabbath is celebrated in heaven so that human beings can imitate the practices of God's angels.

The important point in all our imitation is its deliberate intentionality. We don't just think God's values are good. We embrace them wholly.

15. Embracing Intentionality

YESTERDAY AFTER SUNDAY MORNING WORSHIP three guests came to my home for brunch. After we had finished eating, the woman among my guests immediately began clearing the dishes. I had to ask her not to do that. Since I try to keep the Sabbath by not working, I wanted her to feel free to join me in that celebration. Unfortunately, in our culture we usually derive our sense of personal value by the work that we do. I wanted this special guest to know that she doesn't have to be helpful to be loved and appreciated.

One of the most important aspects of Sabbath keeping is that we embrace intentionality. That phrase emphasizes the value of taking care how we do what we do. If I want to convey to guests in my home the message that they are treasured for who they are and not for what they do, it is important that I be intentional about not letting them work.

Such deliberateness goes against the grain of many Christian lives in twentieth-century America. We so easily fall into the patterns and habits of the world around us in its outrageous lack of commitment that we rarely take time to consider how we do what we do.

Many years ago when I owned a house, a neighbor child came over and walked all through my home—checking out every room. I was curious and asked her what she was searching for. "Your TV," she replied. *"Where* is your TV?"

When I told her I didn't have one, she responded, "Are you *that* poor?" No, I'm not, but I choose not to have a television set. I do not like the values that are espoused in the constant barrage of advertising. I do not want my mind polluted by the explicit genital sexuality that pervades or by the values of home life represented in the stories shown. I agreed with the neighbor girl that there are some good programs on television, but when I want to see those I can go to someone else's house and enjoy fellowship at the same time. I do not want to own a television because for me it would be more destructive than constructive.

My young neighbor could hardly be expected to understand my motivations. However, it is a sad commentary on the state of our society that most families never even question whether having a television set is a good idea. Most families simply own one because everybody else does. It's the thing to do.

Sabbath keeping says clearly that we are not going to do what everybody else does. We are going to be deliberate about our choices in order to live truly as we want to live in response to the grace of God. We are committed to certain values and, therefore, live in accordance with them as fully as we can. Everybody else catches up on yard work on Sundays, but we have chosen to rest from work on our Sabbath day. Everyone else goes window-shopping at the mall on that day, but we have chosen to cease the American hankering after possessions. We embrace the Sabbath day as a holy time for carefulness.

One of the treasures of learning about Sabbath keeping for me has been coming to understand better the Jewish emphasis on acting intentionally. Judaism has often been criticized as a ritualized religion of law, but we must rethink that false notion. Of course, the carefulness of Jewish practices can easily become empty formalism or legalistic duty. On the other hand, we must respect their insistence on practices that set them apart from the culture—not in any elitist, "holier-than-thou" way, but in a way that attempts to prevent their biblical faith and its particular values from being swallowed up by the surrounding culture. Certain values have to be elevated to a higher status in order to separate them from the world.

Chaim Grade, author of *My Mother's Sabbath Days*, tells of a time during his exile in Stalinabad when a man who looked obviously like a Jew approached him. Their conversation vividly illustrates this Jewish intentionality and separation from the surrounding culture:

> "When I saw you wearing that kerchief, I realized at once that this is the Sabbath," I blurt out joyfully. "It never even occurred to me to wonder whether there's an eruv[1] in Stalinabad."
>
> "And before you saw me, you didn't know it is the Sabbath?" He gives me a sidelong glance, and his long, pointed beard, his sharp nose and smoldering eyes, tell me that he is a Hassid, a zealot.
>
> "Indeed, I did sense that it is the Sabbath," I murmur, thinking of my mother's prayer which had so suddenly come to mind [a few moments before this encounter]. "But you know, here one lives in surroundings that do not remind one of the Sabbath. How do you know the proper time for lighting candles, or when to recite Havdalah? There are no Jewish calendars in Russia, are there?"
>
> "Where there's a will, there's a way," he replies with a conspiratorial smile. "There's no law that says a calendar must be printed."
>
> "Oh, a handwritten one? But tell me, how do you avoid violating the Sabbath, since the only day of rest here is on Sunday?"
>
> "Where there's a will, there's a way." And he explains that he is a bookbinder, an independent artisan who works at home and is paid by the piece.
>
> I see that he is about to walk on, but I am unwilling

---

1. An eruv is a wire or fence that translates public space into private domain so that Jews can carry objects within it on the Sabbath day.

to end the conversation. I tell him that I once studied in a yeshiva. He reacts with evident anger and displeasure, looks all about him, and, seeing that the street is deserted, addresses me sternly, slowly, emphasizing each word:

"Since the young man once studied the Torah, he surely knows that the Sabbath is a secret token between the Jewish people and the Master of the Universe. And if the young man has reasons not to reveal his Jewish faith, he should conduct himself like a newly wed couple. When they're among strangers, they communicate with each other by secret signs that no outsider understands, but they understand each other very well. They have their own private tokens of love and affection.

"It seems to me that if I should ever, God forbid, forget when it is the Seventh Day, I would feel the approach of the Holy Day of Rest in my very bones. A good Sabbath to you."

I remain alone on the empty, darkening street and gaze at the crags that tower one above the other. The golden sunset now illumines with a magical glow the blue sky, the crystal-white snow, the green ice on the mountain peaks. Everything melts and burns together in a blaze of diamonds. The purple clouds, the snowcapped mountains, and the bare rocks look like a gigantic city with walls of glass and white towers, where the Sabbath has been rekindled after having been extinguished on earth.[2]

I have quoted this interchange at length because it forces us to ask what price we are willing to pay to remain a community that provides an alternative to society. Since the Enlightenment we have rejected particularism and opted for universalism, but in the moral degeneration and spiritual torpor of our times we must call that attitude into question.

The value of such deliberateness and the fact that it doesn't have to become legalistic or boring are both demonstrated by

---

2. Grade, *My Mother's Sabbath Days: A Memoir*, trans. Channa Kleinerman Goldstein and Inna Hecker Grade (New York: Alfred A. Knopf, 1986), pp. 308-9.

Monet's paintings of the water lilies of Giverny. He painted dozens of canvasses of these plants—each with immense care and intentionality. He didn't have to go far abroad to see subjects to paint; he simply saw more deeply into the pond water at Giverny than anyone else. Each of these canvasses conveys a profound beauty, and each displays a surprising diversity of effects when compared with the others. Similarly, we offer to the world the beauty of our lifestyles when we choose to be careful about each aspect of them. Such intentionality is not legalistic; on the contrary, it frees us to see and make manifest to others in new ways all the lilies of life.

Jacob Neusner's *Invitation to the Talmud* gave me much of my understanding of Sabbath deliberateness. This book explains the development of Talmudic study[3] among the rabbis, whose intensive "logical and rational inquiry is not mere logic-chopping." Rather, it is "a most serious and substantive effort to locate in trivialities the fundamental principles of the revealed will of God to guide and to sanctify the most specific and concrete actions in the workaday world." Neusner's point is that the rabbis sought to imitate God by using their minds. They intended, by their reason and logic, "to carry Torah—revealed teaching—from heaven to earth, and, conversely, to make the profane sacred."[4]

Neusner takes one chapter of the Mishnah that deals with the question of where one should place one's napkin and shows how it was elaborated in the Tosefta, the Palestinian Talmud, and the Babylonian Talmud.[5] Fortunately for us, the chapter that he

---

3. The Talmuds are commentaries on earlier rabbinic works. See footnote 5 for a more complete description.

4. Neusner, *Invitation to the Talmud: A Teaching Book,* rev. ed. (San Francisco: Harper & Row, 1984), pp. xiv-xvii.

5. The Mishnah, from the last quarter of the second century C.E., is the earliest compilation of rabbinic reflection on the Torah. The Tosefta, which means "addition or supplement," elaborates passages from the Mishnah, with or without citing them. The Palestinian Talmud, produced from the third through the fifth centuries, and the Babylonian Talmud, produced between the third and the seventh centuries, are commentaries on the Mishnah and the Tosefta (Neusner, *Invitation to the Talmud,* p. xxvii).

chooses is one directly related to our search for the meaning of Sabbath keeping. The way that Jews pay particular attention on the Sabbath to preparing and eating food according to certain rules much more strict than those normally applied is an example of how they as ordinary people play the role of priests—making their homes sacred places.

Much of this is related to their location in history, their poverty and alienation as exiles. In that misery they imagined a better place, and they kept strict rules to achieve the transformation of their common materials. Neusner aptly summarizes their efforts as follows:

> So how we think changes how things are, and what we think has an effect upon reality. And all of this why? To reaffirm that Israel, the people, attaining cultic cleanness, remains God's holy people—in all its misery and humiliation and disappointment and defeat.[6]

For the Jews, keeping the Sabbath reminded them that their identity was Jewish, that they were able to remain God's holy people in their own homes even if there was no Temple for them to attend to worship Yahweh. In any case, God had first hallowed time, so such a holy place was not necessary, although its restoration would mark their restoration as a people. Perhaps we should give up our church buildings, too, for a while in order to recapture the idea that we are strangers and sojourners on this earth. The Sabbath gives us the opportunity to be in touch with that truth and to re-establish our connections with the eternal instead of being too closely tied up with earthly buildings and our present circumstances.

The paradox is that we are removed from our bond with the material by making the material objects that surround us sacred. By focusing on how we treat our food and our dishes— even on where we put our napkin—we concentrate on holy time.

For me this loosening of the bond with material possessions

---

6. Neusner, *Invitation to the Talmud*, p. 181.

takes place in many deliberate actions, such as cleaning up my house as much as possible on Saturday night so that my home is prepared to welcome Queen Sabbath. Other deliberate actions include carefully arranging things for Sabbath guests the night before so that I don't have to work on the Sabbath day and making everything as pretty as I can in the process; commencing the day with Kiddush; spending extra time in personal and corporate worship; praying as I write letters; choosing carefully which activities I will engage in during the day's celebration; beginning dinner parties with a special prayer to call to mind the meaning of our Sabbath festivities; ending the meal with a prayer to stress the way my guests and I spend our day; and closing the day with Havdalah.

Christianity does not provide an elaborate set of rules to follow for keeping the Sabbath. We all know how those rules became ends in themselves rather than means to an end for some of the Pharisees of Jesus' day. But we ought not to include all the Jews in these faults of overextending the rules and turning them into a means for salvation. Properly understood, the Sabbath rules are not ultra-fussy legislation by which to earn God's favor. Rather, as Neusner teaches us, the Jews' original intention was to be deliberate about their actions in order to recover their identity as the beloved, holy people of God. Similarly, the anthropological study of Jewish culture entitled *Life Is with People* emphasizes that "full observance of the Sabbath prohibitions is more in keeping with the well-beloved and much enjoyed feeling of the Sabbath, the feeling that it is another world, another life, another set of customs."[7]

Christians would do well to follow that kind of intentionality. If we were more deliberate about our lifestyles, we might be more conscious ourselves of God's grace, of who we are as God's people, and of how discipleship involves careful choices. Paying such close attention to living a truly Christian lifestyle would give better witness to the world.

---

7. Mark Zborowski and Elizabeth Herzog, *Life Is with People: The Culture of the Shtetl* (New York: Schocken Books, 1952), p. 51.

This is a tricky balance to maintain. One of the reasons we keep the Sabbath is so that we can learn again to rest as God instructed. But one of the results of learning to rest in our identity as his holy people is a desire to be very careful about how we do what we do in order both to reflect God's grace to others and to deepen our relationship with him. The temptation is great to become legalistic about that intentionality, to turn it into more work. That is why I must be very careful to change what I am doing or how I am observing the Sabbath whenever I find myself feeling burdened by its rules. I find that I generally swing from one extreme to the other. For a while I am better at remembering to be careful about how I do what I do. After that becomes too extremist and graceless, I swing too far in the other direction and lose my deliberateness in the fear of becoming legalistic. Stopping my guest from working to clear the table was a good reminder to me that these days I need to become more deliberate again in my observation of Sabbath keeping.

16. Embracing the Values of the Christian Community

ONE OF THE MAIN REASONS for being deliberate about how we do what we do is so that we can recover more firmly in our lives the different set of values that we hold because we are God's people. Not only do we need to cease the enculturation that so easily entraps us (negative ceasing; see Chapter 6), but also we must positively—and deliberately—choose the values of the kingdom of God. In order to accomplish God's purposes, we recognize a different ordering of priorities, a different mind-set about what is important in and for our lives.

Indeed, we need to become more like the Jews in their uniquely separate distinction from the world if we want to become more truly Christian. *Life Is with People* underscores this sense of the community and its values:

> Not only does each Jew know that all those in the shtetl [small village] are sharing his Sabbath experience. He feels, beyond that, a community with Jews who are celebrating the Sabbath all over the world. This is a major strand in the Sabbath feeling—a sense of proud and joyous identification with the tradition, the past, the ancestors, with all the

111

Jewish world living or gone. On the Sabbath the shtetl feels most strongly and most gladly that "it is good to be a Jew."[1]

How wonderful it would be if we Christians had a greater sense of our global fellowship and of the privilege it is to be a part of the entire tradition of disciples of Jesus. How good it is to be a Christian!

Having a sense of the global Christian community and its unique values entails practical consequences. We saw in the previous section, for example, how our Sabbath keeping is directly related to the whole matter of peace-building. If especially on Sundays we learn and pray to be a people of *shalom,* then throughout the week we will seek to spread that peace throughout the world.

Similarly, as God's people we have a different view of our sexuality. We want to follow God's design for our personhood and deliberately choose his values for genital intercourse only within the protection of a permanent covenantal relationship and of lifelong fidelity in marriage. Lest the youth among us think that notion destroys their freedom to enjoy sex, we must help them to know the true freedom of following God's design in genital intimacy and of choosing the delight of social sexuality and strong, healthy relationships with others that involve various kinds of intimacy other than the genital.

These are some of the values of the Christian community, the ethical concepts based on our roots in the Hebrew Scriptures and taught to us by Jesus and in the epistles of the New Testament. They are not rules hanging over our heads to clobber us if we get out of line, nor means for earning God's favor. Rather, these commands are the instructions by which we learn God's purposes and choose his designs in response to the overwhelming fullness of his love.

The famous sociologist Emile Durkheim labeled "anomie" the social disintegration that has arisen in our times because society lacks a guiding sense of direction. This essentially order-

1. Mark Zborowski and Elizabeth Herzog, *Life Is with People: The Culture of the Shtetl* (New York: Schocken Books, 1952), p. 48.

less character of the contemporary world influences all areas of life as religious and moral restraints lose their effectiveness. Without controls, egoism runs riot—although persons suffering from anomie yearn for some kind of solidarity. Sheldon Wolin brings all of these factors together in this description of the human condition in the modern world:

> Without a stable society, an unquestioned authority, the tight bonds of family, community, vocational group, and religious order, the individual feels lost, beset by an overwhelming sense of loneliness and personal futility.[2]

The choice of God's purposes within the Christian community counteracts the anomie of our society. The grace of God and the continuity of the Church create stability. The Word of God provides the authority. The fellowship of God's people offers tight bonds of intimacy. Within these supports, the individual finds order, solidarity, a sense of direction, and hope.

Another important value in the Christian community is the priority of worship. We choose to spend our time, especially on Sabbath days, in company with others committed to God, remembering our identity as his people together, celebrating our oneness in his grace. During our worship times we praise God and adore him, focus on who he is and try to learn more fully what he is like so that we can imitate him. We hear his Word, his instructions for living as his people, and we rejoice in the delight of his covenant designs. We spend time in prayer, searching for his will and resting in his presence. We choose to meditate on his Word more deeply in Bible classes and in our personal devotional lives, immersing ourselves in his truth so that we might enjoy its freedom.

Worship and devotional times are especially important because they give us the materials for thinking about other dimensions of God's values that we will want to hold together in the Christian community. In an earlier chapter I explained how my

---

2. Wolin, *Politics and Vision: Continuity and Innovation in Western Political Thought* (Boston: Little, Brown, 1960), p. 400.

own values of peace-building came through my study of the Scriptures. All the texts in which Jesus tells us to love our enemies and to feed them continued to haunt me, and I couldn't justify the usual violence with which we deal with those who oppose us.

However, there is still a lot of violence in my life. I discover to my horror that I still want to clobber others intellectually, that my spirit is still often quite competitive rather than cooperative. The Sabbath day is a special holy time for choosing to embrace God's values, for desiring to become like the people he has designed us to be. Often on Sabbath days God performs a special work to bring me to repentance and to conform me more fully to his image.

One of the reasons that I so enjoy reading George MacDonald's novels is that the goodness of his main characters always inspires me to choose those values displayed in the narratives. During the weeks that I was reading a novel of his each Sunday, I was continually challenged to change and felt a deep yearning for God to do more of his transforming work in my life.

The prayer book that I use for daily morning and evening devotions, John Baillie's *Diary of Private Prayer,* contains the following petition as part of its Sunday morning prayer:

> O Thou who art the Source and Ground of all truth, Thou Light of lights, who hast opened the minds of [human beings] to discern the things that are, guide me today, I beseech Thee, in my hours of reading. Give me grace to choose the right books and to read them in the right way. Give me wisdom to abstain as well as to persevere. Let the Bible have proper place; and grant that as I read I may be alive to the stirrings of Thy Holy Spirit in my soul.[3]

I especially appreciate that reminder to want God's guidance even in the choosing of Sabbath books so that what we read might proclaim God's values and so that, by the Holy Spirit, our souls might be stirred and transformed to choose those values.

---

3. Baillie, *A Diary of Private Prayer* (New York: Charles Scribner's Sons, 1949), p. 133.

Baillie's evening prayer then shows how the Sabbath choosing of values can carry over into all the other days of the week. This is how the prayer concludes:

> Grant, O heavenly Father, that the spiritual refreshment I have this day enjoyed may not be left behind and forgotten as tomorrow I return to the cycle of common tasks. Here is a fountain of inward strength. Here is a purifying wind that must blow through all my business and all my pleasures. Here is light to enlighten all my road. Therefore, O God, do Thou enable me so to discipline my will that in hours of stress I may honestly seek after those things for which I have prayed in hours of peace.[4]

The grace of Sabbath refreshment and the consequent deliberateness of Sabbath contemplation and prayer can thus be carried over into the week in the ways in which we act on the values of the Christian community in every aspect of our lives.

Baillie's morning naming of God as "the Source and Ground of all truth" and the "Light of lights" reminds us also that our choosing of God's values is possible only because God's grace enlightens and guides and leads us to a deliberate rejection of the values of the culture around us. In a society that chooses promiscuity, we intentionally pursue faithfulness and chastity. In an age that chooses materialism, we deliberately seek to share with those in need. In a world that chooses violence, we take care to build peace and to be agents of reconciliation wherever possible. Indeed, these values can be known only by the enlightenment of God's Spirit. Such spiritual things are accessible only to those who can spiritually discern them. Therefore, we need a day devoted to the One True Light, as well as daily time deliberately spent in his company, in order to receive and embrace the truth he reveals.

I have titled this chapter "Embracing the Values of the Christian Community" and have frequently referred to our gathering

---

4. Baillie, *A Diary of Private Prayer*, p. 135.

together in worship. But I also need to make deliberate note of the value of being a community together, because in that respect the Church in the twentieth century generally fails horribly to embrace God's design.

The members of the early Christian Church were known for their frequent gathering together, for sharing all their possessions in common, for their constant adherence to the teaching of the apostles, for fellowship (in the full meaning of that word), and for communal praying and breaking of bread. They were continually devoted to these practices; they were committed to them and frequently engaged in them. They loved to be together, and they celebrated their community with glad and generous hearts (Acts 2:42-47).

Indeed, Acts 2:42-47 confronts us with the following set of values:

- being continually devoted to our relationship as a community;
- wanting more than anything else to have our lives guided by the instruction of God's Word;
- sharing deeply in each other's needs and carrying one another's burdens, since the true meaning of fellowship is "having in common";
- gathering together for the breaking of the bread and thereby "discerning the Body of Christ," which means to care for the poor, to eliminate class distinctions between the people of our world;
- spending time in earnest prayer for one another and for the needs of the larger community and the world;
- owning possessions in common so that we have more resources to share with those in need;
- meeting regularly in the temple as well as in each other's homes to share meals with gladness;
- experiencing signs and wonders among us.

This is quite a challenging list. Some of the values on it we have already explored in previous chapters, and some we will explore later in this book. At this point we will focus especially on the whole idea of choosing to be together—an idea for which we certainly need to catch a new vision!

In most congregations it is painfully true that the members gather only for worship and then quickly disperse to their own tasks and pleasures. One of the special meanings of Sabbath keeping for me has been the notion that the Christian community *gathers* on that day. If our Sabbath days become set aside for spiritual purposes and set apart from work and productivity, we can afford to spend more time together with our fellow believers so that we can be more thoroughly strengthened in the values of the community. One of the reasons that teenagers find it so hard to be Christians today is that they experience so little support from the Christian community and have to contend with so many worldly values—concerning faith, materialism, their sexuality, and drugs and alcohol. Of course, it is possible for a person to remain faithful to Christian values even if she or he stands alone. However, if we could more fully enfold our youth in our communities so that they felt profoundly loved and thoroughly supported, they might find it much less difficult to choose the values of the Christian community as their own, despite the pressures of their peers.

We can gather together for all sorts of things when we observe Sabbath keeping. Not only will we meet for worship and Bible classes, but perhaps we can have meals together. Breaking bread together might also give us an opportunity to serve the larger community. Broadway Christian Parish in South Bend, Indiana, hosts family dinners for the neighborhood after worship on Sunday. During my last year there I immensely enjoyed lending a hand to the weekly crew that prepared dinner for all the neighbors who came. In this way we served the poor, but not in a way that would destroy the dignity of those who received our gifts. Rather, we had a family meal together—the congregation and the neighborhood. The most delightful aspect of the whole program was that many of the neighborhood children also participated in the worship and Sunday school that preceded our meal together. Several times a few black children became my family during the worship hour, and their friendship was an utter delight for me.

Perhaps our Christian communities can gather together for special extra times of worship. Since my move to Washington I have searched for Sunday-evening Advent services held by Lutheran congregations, and I have been distressed to find none. Those special times of preparation for the coming of the Christ Child were favorite worship times for me when I was a child, and I wish I could enjoy them with some Christian community here in my new hometown.

Perhaps we can gather together in smaller fellowship clusters as part of our Sabbath keeping. Some congregations have such fellowship groups that extend the Christian community into the week. These caring groups offer further opportunities for Bible study, sharing, encouragement, and prayer.

Perhaps we can enjoy wintertime activities like skating and sledding, summer swims and ball games, long bike rides, picnics, hikes, or trips. Maybe some of us can enjoy a movie with the teenagers in our community and then discuss it afterward in order to nourish the youth in our Christian values as opposed to the cultural values they confront. Those of us who play musical instruments can have jam sessions to praise God or even produce a concert together.

My whole point is that to be a Christian community together we need time together. Observing the Sabbath gives us the intentional time for deepening the bonds of our community and enfolding each of us more foundationally in the values that we share.

17. Embracing Time
instead of Space

ONE OF THE SPECIFIC CHOICES among the values of the Christian community is the embracing of time instead of space. We must return to the question of how we in our busy lives can afford to spend a whole day in Sabbath ceasing, resting, embracing, and feasting when it seems we don't have enough time to do what has to be done. Surrounded as we are by the rapid pace of too much change, we think we cannot set aside such time. However, when we take the day to assess our use of time, we learn what is important in all those changes and how to prioritize our tasks and desires so that we aren't overcome by the tyranny of the urgent. We must develop an objective perspective (rather than thinking we are "out of time") to assess the quality of our days. This perspective has many aspects, but one of the foremost is the deliberate decision to focus on events in time with persons rather than using time to acquire or accomplish things.

One of my favorite stories from the Gospels is this account of Jesus healing a crippled woman on the Sabbath day:

> On a Sabbath Jesus was teaching in one of the synagogues, and a woman was there who had been crippled by a spirit

for eighteen years. She was bent over and could not straighten up at all. When Jesus saw her, he called her forward and said to her, "Woman, you are set free from your infirmity." Then he put his hands on her, and immediately she straightened up and praised God.

Indignant because Jesus had healed on the Sabbath, the synagogue ruler said to the people, "There are six days for work. So come and be healed on those days, not on the Sabbath."

The Lord answered him, "You hypocrites! Doesn't each of you on the Sabbath untie his ox or donkey from the stall and lead it out to give it water? Then should not this woman, a daughter of Abraham, whom Satan has kept bound for eighteen long years, be set free on the Sabbath day from what bound her?"

When he said this, all his opponents were humiliated, but the people were delighted with all the wonderful things he was doing. (Luke 13:10-17)

I am always struck by the exuberance of this story and by the exhilaration I feel in response to the way it reveals Jesus' embracing of the true meaning of the Sabbath.

In the first place, we notice that Jesus honored the Sabbath. He spent it worshiping and teaching. However, because he truly embraced time instead of space, he cherished persons more than rules. Noticing a woman who had been bent over double for eighteen years (Luke is very precise in his description), Jesus called her forward—a most unusual thing for a Jewish rabbi to do! For him the time was well spent in setting this woman free from the bondage of physical infirmity and the social, emotional, and spiritual bondage that went along with her affliction.

What good news he announced to her—that she had been set free! The form of the Greek verb that records his proclamation emphasizes that since she had been decisively set free, she would remain free. Moreover, Jesus touched her—and that truly set her free.

In the opinion of many Jews at that time (and, unfortunately, in the opinion of many Christians today who insist that true believers *must* be healed), physical illness was (is) a manifestation of spiritual impurity. (That is why the disciples ask Jesus in John 9:2, "Rabbi, who sinned, this man or his parents, that he was born blind?") Furthermore, if a person was impure, anyone who touched him or her would become impure also. Consequently, this woman probably hadn't been touched for eighteen years! Imagine the pain and isolation of that. By his gentle touch, Jesus affirmed her spiritually and socially, offered her emotional healing, and restored her fully to the worshiping community. The Greek text underscores the extent of both her healing (saying that immediately she was "rebuilt") and her praising (since the Greek verb form emphasizes its continuation). She was rebuilt in every aspect of her being and knew that the credit belonged to God.

There is a great deal of humor in the responses that follow Jesus' healing of the woman. The synagogue leader is upset, but afraid to confront Jesus directly, so he speaks to the crowds about the six days on which work—and healing—should be done. Jesus, however, knows that others besides the leader are bothered by his action, so he responds with the plural "hypocrites!" Then he points to their mixed-up sense of values. Don't they untie their animals to let them get a drink of water on the Sabbath? Then surely this "daughter of Abraham" (a good Jew, just as they are good Jews) ought to be set free from her affliction. The bystanders, of course, are utterly delighted with Jesus. He has humiliated the pompous prigs who opposed him.

In that final comment, however, there lies a treacherous trap. Too easily we identify with the crowd and rejoice in the shaming of our enemies, without realizing that our very identification with the lowly proves that we are pompous prigs, too. Do we really rejoice at God's restoration of the humble? Is our love as impartial as God's—or do we think that others should at least be a little more worthy before receiving God's grace?

Do our Sabbath practices—and our actions on other days

as well--set others free from the things that put them into bondage? Jesus embraced a woman who was socially unacceptable and set her free. He offers a model of how we can keep the Sabbath by embracing persons rather than rules or things.

If we are cherishing time rather than space, we know that Sabbath keeping means an investment in individuals instead of in possessions and accomplishments. In fact, we use those very possessions to celebrate persons and life. Liberating growth takes time, so, if we want to experience personal growth and set others free, we need ample time for the processes of change.

One of the delights of Sabbath practices for me is that ceasing our work and concentrating on spiritual resting create the possibility for deeper caring about the persons whom God brings into our day. There is no need to hurry—for there is nothing that we *have to do*. There are no tasks that demand our time. Time is a gift to us, and we can in turn pass that gift on to others. Moreover, if we are resting in grace, then we can enfold others in its freedom, too.

Another delight is that when we spend time embracing persons, we discover many new and wonderful things about them. God always seems to have many pleasant surprises in store for us when we are committed to observing the Sabbath and acknowledging that he is Master of our time.

I remember especially one summer Sabbath afternoon at a camp in Iowa. I had been looking forward to a day of deep rest after a very tiring week of teaching high-school students. I went out to the dock at the lake, but, instead of enjoying a long-awaited nap, I spent a much more restful afternoon in conversation with some of the camp staff members—college-aged counselors who were really growing in their faith. Conversing with them was wonderfully renewing for my own faith, and extra sleep came later.

The delight of embracing time rather than things is that we are free from the bondage of a schedule. Gifts can happen whenever they come, and we are not bound to certain times for certain experiences. Furthermore, if we freely give our time, we will harvest it in greater abundance. Dorothy Day, founder of the Catholic Worker movement, writes about the principle of sowing time and thereby reaping it. If we spend an hour in worship and prayer, we will have more time than ever because we will spend what we have with clarity, and our work will get done. She especially counsels that we lavishly sow time by truly *listening* to the poor.[1]

During the past few years in graduate school, I loved the freedom I had on Sabbath days to visit with others and not feel the pressure of having to get home to read a book or finish a paper. I had the whole day free to enjoy the individuals who participated in Sabbath keeping with me by going to concerts or sharing meals and conversation. Certainly we can always enjoy other people more fully when no obligations are impinging on our time.

In our society it is difficult to embrace people instead of things, to cherish time rather than space. So much of our technologically efficient and materially exploitative culture militates against these values. Accordingly, we must, by deliberate effort, consciously establish our intentions. Moreover, if we keep the Sabbath by embracing persons, that practice invites us to carry those same values into the other six days of the week. Our Sabbath remembering strengthens us to stand against the technologization of our culture and pursue the intimacy of Christian community and Christ-like caring.

Furthermore, when we experience being enveloped by Sabbath time, we become people who are not enslaved to time. As we embrace time, then, we squander less and less of it for the things of space. We get in touch with eternity and bring eternal values into all the days of our week.

---

1. Day, *The Long Loneliness: An Autobiography* (San Francisco: Harper & Row, 1981), p. 252.

18. Embracing Giving
instead of Requiring

ONE OF THE WORST THINGS our acquisitive society has done to the Christian faith is that it has turned our major holy days into commercialized holidays, days of "gimme" instead of special times of adoration and worship. Even children from the most devout homes cannot escape the cultural conditioning—the Santas in all the stores asking what they want for Christmas, the displays of toys and decorations appearing even before Halloween, and now even the advertisements about what toys to demand for Easter.

Perhaps the Christian community could repel this invasion with a weekly counteroffensive—the Sabbath practice of giving rather than accumulating, of caring for the needs of others instead of requiring for oneself, of putting aside one's personal pleasure in order to create pleasure for many. Especially for the sake of our children, we want to model the importance of embracing a lifestyle of giving; for our own sake, we adults need the freedom that inevitably results from choosing to be stewards rather than possessors.

Our negative ceasing to possess must be accompanied by a positive choosing to be generous. Not only do we give up the consumerism and accumulation and exploitation of our society (see Chapter 5), but also we release ourselves from burdens by sharing our material and spiritual possessions—the food from our tables, the flowers from our gardens, the music in our souls.

The apostle Paul set the pattern for Christians when he wrote in his first letter to the church at Corinth,

> Now about the collection for God's people: Do what I told the Galatian churches to do. On the first day of every week, each one of you should set aside a sum of money in keeping with his income, saving it up, so that when I come no collections will have to be made. (1 Cor. 16:1-2)

That really was a tremendous bit of wisdom: if everyone sets aside a proportionate amount of his or her income, there would be plenty in store when the time came to gather the offerings to help the victims of the famine in Jerusalem. Moreover, the text emphasizes that the setting aside was done in connection with observing the day of worship, for to the early Christians "the first day of the week" emphasized the resurrection of their Lord and suggested that what was done on that day came in response to the miracle of that event.

In his second letter to the Corinthians, Paul expanded this invitation to contribute. Rejoicing in the generosity of the Macedonian churches, he challenged the believers at Corinth to the same earnestness and gave this advice in 2 Corinthians 8:11-15 and 9:6-15:

> Now finish the work, so that your eager willingness to do it may be matched by your completion of it, according to your means. For if the willingness is there, the gift is acceptable according to what one has, not according to what he does not have.
>
> Our desire is not that others might be relieved while you are hard pressed, but that there might be equality. At the present time your plenty will supply what they need, so that in turn their plenty will supply what you need. Then there will be equality, as it is written: "He that gathered

much did not have too much, and he that gathered little did not have too little." (cf. Exod. 16:18)

. . . Remember this: Whoever sows sparingly will also reap sparingly, and whoever sows generously will also reap generously. Each [person] should give what he has decided in his heart to give, not reluctantly or under compulsion, for God loves a cheerful giver. And God is able to make all grace abound to you, so that in all things at all times, having all that you need, you will abound in every good work. As it is written:

"He has scattered abroad his gifts to the poor;
his righteousness endures forever." (cf. Ps. 112:9)

Now he who supplies seed to the sower and bread for food will also supply and increase your store of seed and will enlarge the harvest of your righteousness. You will be made rich in every way so that you can be generous in every occasion, and through us your generosity will result in thanksgiving to God.

This service that you perform is not only supplying the needs of God's people but is also overflowing in many expressions of thanks to God. Because of the service by which you have proved yourselves, [people] will praise God for the obedience that accompanies your confession of the gospel of Christ, and for your generosity in sharing with them and with everyone else. And in their prayers for you their hearts will go out to you, because of the surpassing grace God has given you. Thanks be to God for his indescribable gift!

In challenging the Corinthians to Sabbath giving, Paul urged them to make their gifts to the poor as a fulfillment of their own goals—not according to any prescribed regulations, but according to their own individual means. Notice the freedom of that in contrast to rigid Christian tithes or Jewish rules. Unfortunately, such a freedom in the church often degenerates into the notion that we can give skimpily because we are not required to pay a certain amount. But Paul's exhortation follows his reminder of the example of the Macedonians, who were undergoing the "most severe trial," and yet "their overflowing joy and their extreme poverty welled up in rich generosity. For I testify that they gave as much as they were able, and even beyond their ability" (2 Cor. 8:2). This is the most unusual equation in the history of humanity:

$$\text{most severe trial} + \text{overflowing Joy} + \text{extreme poverty} = \text{rich generosity!}$$

What a tremendous model of caring for the needy. Paul established equality as the criterion, that those who have might supply the needs of those who have not; when the roles are reversed, those who were once "haves" are supported by those who were once "have nots." Paul quoted a passage from Exodus to verify this principle, which connects us again to the practice of Sabbath keeping, because the fact that each Israelite gathering manna had exactly what he or she needed ties in very closely with the command not to gather manna on the Sabbath, but to trust that there would be enough. (See the previous discussion of Exod. 16:21-38 in Chapter 4.)

Furthermore, Paul reminded the Corinthians that generous giving leads to rich reaping. Of course, that slogan ought not to be turned into a "claim," as is frequently done in contemporary Christianity—that, if we do our part, God is required to reward us with abundant material blessings. Such a heresy is not biblically warranted, for it reverses the cause and effect. The point is not that if we sow generously God has to respond with abundant blessings. On the contrary, because he has already blessed us abundantly, we are able to be generous in our giving. The fact is that we can never outgive God, but in no way does that give us leave to demand from him!

Good stewardship in the biblical sense lies in recognizing that God gives us all that we need to abound in good works and in trusting him to provide what is needed for the ministries to which he has called us. I am always surprised—although I know I shouldn't be—by the way that promise works out in fact. Throughout the months that Christians Equipped for Ministry (the organization under which I free-lance) sponsored a home to welcome women in crisis, we never lacked the necessary food to feed all those who came. Similarly, in my experiences with soup kitchens and Catholic Worker houses (shelters that care for the poor), somehow God always provides what is needed to abound in good works, "which God prepared in advance for us to do" (Eph. 2:10).

Paul continued his letter with the image that God increases our store of seed so that we can be generous. A friend of mine always grows extra rows of potatoes and other vegetables in his garden so that he can take the surplus produce to the local food bank. He can attest to God's increasing the seed so that plenty can be grown.

The benefits that come from generosity are much more than material ones, however. Paul rejoiced that the Corinthians' contributions to the needs of others would result in overflowing expressions of thanks to God. Certainly this is one of the most delightful of all the blessings that come from giving: the deepening of the faith of those who receive.

I experienced that profoundly many years ago on the receiving end. I had become convinced that it would be best to buy a large, three-story house in Olympia (Washington) to establish the C.E.M. home for women in crisis. The problem was that I needed a large down payment in order to buy into the previous owner's mortgage, and, even though I had already cashed in all my bonds and borrowed everything that my parents could lend me, I still didn't have enough funds. I was teaching in Anchorage, Alaska, just a few days before the down payment had to be made, and I asked the people there if anyone could lend me money that I would repay with interest as soon as possible. One family generously lent a large amount, but I was still $500 short of the total I needed.

As it happened, that week in Alaska included my birthday, and on that evening, after I was done teaching, the secretary of the congregation motioned me into her office to hand me an envelope that she had found that day on her desk. A little card inside said, "Have the happiest birthday, Marva" and was signed, "Someone who loves you." And inside that envelope were ten $100 bills!

To this day I have never found out who gave me that generous gift. Not only did it complete the down payment, but also it supplied extra money to recarpet the basement to turn it into a bedroom and office for me. To this day I have never ceased to give thanks for my anonymous benefactor. At that time his or her gift reassured me that it was indeed according to God's purposes to purchase the large house and establish the ministry. My faith was immeasurably deepened, and that strengthening proved to be especially important during the times when we doubted the work that we were trying to do in that house. Simply recalling how God had miraculously provided for its purchase increased our confidence and trust in the work he wanted to do through us in that place.

Paul also wrote of the obedience that accompanies our confession of the gospel. That seems to me to be one of the most important challenges for our Sabbath giving. If we say that on the Sabbath day we cease working in order to demonstrate that we trust God to provide for our needs and security, we can practice that trust by means of our own generosity. The proclamation of the gospel, the faith that God's love frees us to love, is made more credible when it is tangibly accompanied by works of love and obedience to God's covenant instructions to care for the needy.

Finally, to give generously deepens the bonds of the Christian community. As Paul emphasized to the Corinthians, the hearts of the poor in Jerusalem who received their aid would go out to the Greek church; the believers in one place would pray for those in another. Jesus told us that where our money is, that is where our hearts are also (Luke 12:34). If we are involved in giving to various mission concerns and ministries, we will inevitably be involved in prayer for their work, even as the recipients will pray in gratitude for our support. A special part of our Sabbath prayers can include the various mission agencies or persons in ministry whom we support with our finances.

Sabbath giving, of course, includes much more than money. Jewish people still give flowers or wrapped gifts to loved ones as part of their Sabbath celebrations. I like to use the day to make valentines, write letters, or crochet or bake things to give as presents. We will outline more aspects of these practices in the following section on feasting, for certainly one of the ways in which we create and celebrate a festival is by the delight of giving to others on Sabbath days.

One last point in Paul's exhortation is especially significant. To conclude his comments on stewardship, he thanked God for "his indescribable gift." We assume that this phrase refers to the gift of salvation, since earlier Paul had written of "the grace of our Lord Jesus Christ, that though he was rich, yet for your sakes he became poor, so that you through his poverty might become rich" (2 Cor. 8:9).

To keep the Sabbath is to focus on the immensity of God's gifts to us, especially the priceless gift of salvation. We can respond in no other way than to want to give in similar fashion. "Christ's love compels us . . ." (2 Cor. 5:14a).

19. Embracing Our Calling in Life

SOME DAYS I RESENT BEING SINGLE. I get tired of having to come home from speaking engagements to a cold, empty house. I wish there was someone with whom I could share all the little things that make life special.

Whenever I am being faithful in observing the Sabbath, however, those resentments dissolve. To dwell on who God is and who I am in light of his character always leads me to sheer gratitude for the privilege of my own unique position as his servant. Just as there are disadvantages both to being married and to being single, there are advantages on both sides: both marriage and singleness include special channels for God's grace and unique opportunities to serve God. The Sabbath is a day for counting our blessings and embracing the goodness of our own particular circumstances.

One of my best friends and I have a little joke about that. Whenever I spend time with Tim, I am extraordinarily comforted by the depth of his faith and his caring, but I also often say that I could not endure what he has to go through because of kidney failure. (He is tied three days a week to a dialysis machine and limited on other days by problems with blood pressure and the sludginess that comes from too many waste products in his blood.) In turn, Tim always says that he wouldn't want to deal with *my* physical handicaps. Being together always leaves both of us more grateful for our own particular calling in life.

After a day of genuine Sabbath keeping (I use the word *genuine* because some days I am simply not very good at observing the Sabbath), I always am reduced to repentance for my complaining spirit. Inevitably the day impresses me with the goodness of God, and invariably it increases my longing to be more faithful in serving God according to the gifts and resources he has given and the calling he has issued. The time spent in worship and with other members of the Christian community, the time devoted to solitude and prayer, the special times of hosting dinner parties or looking at art or participating in music—however my day is spent, its components contribute together to fill me with gratitude for God's immeasurable gifts.

The Sabbath is not only a day to increase our gratitude for the particular gifts of our situations; Sabbath keeping also gives us a holy time for actually discovering as well as embracing more thoroughly our calling in life. This is implied in Psalm 92, which is entitled "A psalm. A song. For the Sabbath day." The declarations of this psalm reveal some of the practices in the worship of the Hebrew people:

> It is good to praise the LORD
>   and make music to your name, O Most High,
> to proclaim your love in the morning
>   and your faithfulness at night,
> to the music of the ten-stringed lyre
>   and the melody of the harp.
>
> For you make me glad by your deeds, O LORD;
>   I sing for joy at the works of your hands.
> How great are your works, O LORD,
>   how profound your thoughts!
> The senseless [person] does not know,
>   fools do not understand,

that though the wicked spring up like grass
    and all evildoers flourish,
they will be forever destroyed.

But you, O LORD, are exalted forever.

For surely your enemies, O LORD,
    surely your enemies will perish,
    all evildoers will be scattered.
You have exalted my horn like that of a wild ox;
    fine oils have been poured upon me.
My eyes have seen the defeat of my adversaries;
    my ears have heard the rout of my wicked foes.

The righteous will flourish like a palm tree,
    they will grow like a cedar of Lebanon;
planted in the house of the LORD,
    they will flourish in the courts of our God.
They will still bear fruit in old age,
    they will stay fresh and green,
proclaiming, "The LORD is upright;
    he is my Rock, and there is no wickedness in him."

All the practices mentioned in the first stanza of this Sabbath psalm invite our Sunday imitation—praising Yahweh, making music, proclaiming God's love and faithfulness. Then the rest of the verses give several hints that Sabbath keeping makes us more able to embrace our particular callings.

In the second stanza the poet rejoices in Yahweh's deeds; he sings for Joy, in fact, because of God's works. Since senseless persons and fools are not aware of God's deeds and do not understand them, they do not realize that their lifestyle leads to futility, that although it seems to flourish it will in the end be destroyed. On the contrary, those who are God's people recognize that their lives are part of the larger purposes of God, that Yahweh's works are great, that his wisdom is profound.

In *The Mustard Seed Conspiracy*, Tom Sine emphasizes that we ask the wrong question if we search for God's will in our lives. He says that we should instead see what God is doing in the world and become part of his program.[1] This is the implication of the psalm, for, in contrast to those fools whose lives are futile, the people of God are made glad in thinking about his works and purposes. They rejoice in the fact that Yahweh is exalted forever.

Their own participation in God's purposes is implied more strongly in the next stanza, when the poet declares that Yahweh has exalted his horn (which means strength) and that fine oils have been poured upon him. For the Hebrew people, anointing with oil signified a commissioning for the special purposes of God. Kings were anointed, as were priests. Oil was a symbol of God's flowing blessings, but it also indicated a connection with God's assignment.

Finally, the poet declares in the last stanza that the righteous flourish and continue to grow like palm trees and the cedars of Lebanon. Even in old age, the people of God will bear fruit and stay "fresh and green" because of Yahweh's continued presence in their lives. Because of Yahweh's uprightness, because he is their Rock, in whom there is no wickedness, the righteous will continue to flourish.

Reflecting upon God's character during Sabbath days always incites me to renewed zeal for his purposes, a holy restlessness in my desire to serve him more effectively, yet a deep contentment in how I can serve. For example, thinking about Jesus as the Prince of Peace makes me want to be more of a peace-builder. I become more discontent with the violent nature of our society and more eager to serve as an agent of reconciliation in the local—and even the global—community. The more I contemplate his character of love and healing, the more I want to be like him. Thus, to keep the Sabbath always deepens my understanding of, and enthusiasm for, his call in my life.

Various Sabbath activities contribute to this end. In worship the Scripture lessons and sermon and prayers often give us clear instruction for ways to fulfill our calling. For example, a prayer

---

1. Sine, *The Mustard Seed Conspiracy* (Waco, Tex.: Word Books, 1981).

for a congregational member who is ill might spark insight into how we can serve as care-givers—visiting, bringing flowers, preparing food, sending cards. Similarly, the Holy Spirit uses our personal Bible study, meditation, and prayer to reveal to us and develop in us the character of God.

In addition, quality time spent with others in conversation and prayer often strengthens our own notion of who we are and what we are to do with our lives. Moreover, in the moments of ceasing work and the need to accomplish we can get more fully in touch with who we truly are, and that helps us know the resources with which God created us in order that his purposes could be uniquely fulfilled in our lives. Sometimes my Sabbath reading (especially when I'm reading a fairy tale or a George MacDonald novel) stirs up in me a great longing to put into action some particular dimension of my personality. For example, stories often invite me to pay more attention to my right-brained, creative, artistic, poetic side—which sometimes gets lost in the left-brained analytical work of the weekdays.

Above all, we realize in our Sabbath keeping that God's love is to be proclaimed in the world. Each of us has certain gifts and personality traits that contribute uniquely to that proclamation. Some people are superb singers, and others are quiet listeners. Some people give wise counsel, and others more easily give affection. All of those gifts and all of our personalities are needed to tell the world all that God wants to say about himself. The strengthening that we experience on the Sabbath day empowers us to use those particular resources during the week to communicate God's love in our specific fashion to those around us.

I especially want to emphasize in connection with this chapter that I entitled this section "Embracing" rather than "Choosing" (which was my original title) because I realized as I worked that I needed a stronger word to convey the intensity with which we grasp the positive aspects of Sabbath keeping. That we choose something doesn't necessarily mean that we incorporate it thoroughly into our lives. To embrace is to accept with gusto, to live to the hilt, to choose with extra intentionality and tenacity.

Part of the weakness of our Christian witness stems from the fact that often it is so lackadaisical, so lackluster. The early Christians set their world on fire with the exuberance of their Joy. We might not necessarily be happy in the particular circumstances of the moment, but we can always know Joy because the Resurrection is an accomplished fact. We can be sure "that our present sufferings are not worth comparing with the glory that will be revealed in us" and "that in all things God works for the good of those who love him, who have been called according to his purpose" (Rom. 8:18, 28). Furthermore, we can be confident that nothing will ever be able to separate us from the love of God in Christ Jesus (Rom. 8:38-39). These unfailing assurances lead us to profound Joy. Everyone in the world is looking for such confidence and hope, and each of us is particularly suited for sharing it with those whom we encounter in our daily worlds.

We can embrace our calling to share God's love with the exhilaration of knowing that God has uniquely equipped each of us for our particular roles and that he will provide all that we need for the ministry to which he has called us. Immersing ourselves in his love on the Sabbath overwhelms us with his grace, clarifies our perceptions of our role, and empowers us for the tasks that he makes clear.

20. Embracing
Wholeness—Shalom

SOMETIMES WHEN WE ARE REALLY TIRED, we long desperately just for some "peace and quiet"—by which we mean the absence of hassle and conflict. Unfortunately, however, because we use the word *peace* in such a connotation, we have let the word degenerate into simply another designation for relief.

God wants much more for us. The peace that he wants to give us goes far beyond merely an absence of conflict. As we noted in Chapter 8, the Hebrew word for peace, *shalom,* begins in reconciliation with God and continues in reconciliation with our sisters and brothers—even our enemies. Moreover, *shalom* designates being at peace with ourselves, health, wealth, fulfillment, satisfaction, contentment, tranquility, and—to sum it all up—wholeness.

We have discussed many aspects of Sabbath wholeness in previous chapters of this book. In particular, the chapters on physical, spiritual, emotional, and intellectual rest have pointed out the ways that we find integrity in each dimension of our being through a day of rest. Our spirits become more unified when our relationship with God is the center and focus of our lives and all other aspects find their proper priorities in the worship of the Lord. Our bodies are more sound when we enjoy a rhythm of fasting and feasting (which will be explored in Chapter 25), when we truly rest by giving up the burden of possessions, when we have time for naps. Our souls are more complete when we can get in touch with our deepest emotions, our true sexuality, our creativity, our senses of delight and play. Our minds become more robust when the narratives of our heritage as God's people remind us of our redemption and when, as a result, our attitudes are made more wholesome and our freedom leads to the generating of new ideas.

Furthermore, the interworking of all these aspects of our beings finds a new unity in Sabbath keeping because we no longer dichotomize between mind and matter, our bodies and our spirits or souls, our left and right brains. Rather, all becomes sacred and wholly integrated in our distinction from the world. We have even seen that there ceases to be any dichotomy between solitude and communal togetherness, because each is necessary for the other, and each contributes to the fullness of our being in relationship with God. As we become more intentional both about being a gathered Christian community and about enjoying our special times of solitude with God, the two work together to create a greater sense of both individual and corporate wholeness.

One of the ways in which the Sabbath contributes to our wholeness is that it frees us to enjoy all the dimensions of our being. As we enjoy art or music and appreciate beauty, as we experience the healing and rediscovery of our emotions, as we celebrate our true masculinity and femininity, these things bring greater balance to our lives. Moreover, in the integration that thorough ceasing, resting, embracing, and feasting produce, we know our real identity, and that leads to the genuine humility and confidence of truth.

Perhaps the most important aspect of Sabbath keeping that contributes immensely to wholeness in our human existence is the prevalence of order. We crave order to give us a sense that things are under control, that we can cope with whatever might be happening because it fits into a larger plan. That is why the keeping of the Sabbath rhythm is so important: the orderly cycle of six days of work and one day of resting and embracing God's values matches the rhythm of our creation, which God has revealed to us in the Scriptures.

Throughout their scriptural narratives, both the Hebrew people and the early Christians underline the sevenfold rhythm built into our innermost beings. We are probably all aware of the prevalence of sevens in the Book of Revelation, the letters of Paul, and the Gospel of John, but the septenary structure of Genesis 1:1–2:3 is less obvious in our English translations. The Hebrew account is composed of seven sections; verse one contains seven words; verse two contains fourteen words. Many words occur in multiples of seven—the words *God, earth, the heavens,* and *light* occur 35, 21, 21, and 7 times, respectively. In addition, Genesis 2:2-3 has three sentences of seven Hebrew words each, and the middle word in each sentence is the word for *seventh day,* used to emphasize this as the goal of creation.[1]

It is very interesting to note that over time the world's civilizations have implemented various patterns for the cycle of work and rest. We read in history of the Babylonian market days that were held every first, seventh, fifteenth, and twenty-eighth days. Other civilizations have tried four, five, six, eight, and even ten-day weeks, but no pattern other than a seven-day week has persisted through time. Indeed, the rhythm of seven days was known even to the early Phoenicians,[2] and Robert North, author of "The Derivation of Sabbath," adds that it was also common for Babylonians, Egyptians, Persians, Indians, Chinese, Mongols, Malays, Germans, Greeks, and the Cherokees and other Native Americans. The world has discovered that a seven-day week matches our inmost being, yet, North asserts, "the adaptation of various ancient elements into an invariably-recurrent sabbath of

---

1. Samuele Bacchiocchi, *Divine Rest for Human Restlessness: A Theological Study of the Good News of the Sabbath for Today* (Rome: Pontifical Gregorian University Press, 1980), pp. 17-76.

2. Henri Cazelles, *Études sur le Code de l'Alliance* (Paris: Letouzey et Ané, 1946), p. 94.

highly purified observance was an original and immensely in-fluential cultural achievement of the Mosaic revelation."[3]

A further ordering by the Sabbath occurs when individuals or groups develop certain customs that they follow every week. Whether or not I have company and what activities I might choose to do will vary from week to week, but certain things do not change. Every week I begin the Sabbath with Kiddush prayers and candles, spend some time in worship and Bible study, eat different foods from those of the rest of the week, and end the Sabbath celebration with candles and the Havdalah (farewell) prayers.

The Jews, too, made certain customs a part of every Sab-bath celebration. This goes all the way back to the beginnings of their observances, as it is recorded in Leviticus 24. The twelve loaves of shewbread, representing each of the twelve tribes, were to be "set out before the LORD regularly, Sabbath after Sabbath, on behalf of the Israelites, as a lasting covenant" (v. 8). When there was no longer a tabernacle or a temple, the Jews brought the Sabbath customs into their own homes—perceiving them as holy places and the fathers of the households as the priests—to continue in practices designating themselves as the holy people of God. As Brevard Childs, the author of *The Book of Exodus*, em-phasizes, "The tabernacle represents the fulfillment of the cove-nant promise, 'I will make my dwelling with you. . . . I will be your God and you shall be my people.' But the actual sign of the covenant is the sabbath."[4]

We Christians, too, can establish certain regular customs for Sabbath days. By observing them on a constant basis, we give order to our lives, although we want to be careful lest such cus-toms degenerate into dull routines and onerous legalistic bur-dens. We want our worship to be a delightful habit, not the empty ritual of "going to church"!

---

3. North, "The Derivation of Sabbath," *Biblica* 36 (1955): 201.
4. Childs, *The Book of Exodus: A Critical, Theological Commentary* (Philadelphia: Westminster Press, 1974), p. 541.

The most important ordering takes place in our lives when we observe the Sabbath focus of placing God at the center and then prioritize everything else in proper relation to that focus. Keeping the Sabbath day constantly reminds us that Yahweh is to be pre-eminent in our lives.

Furthermore, this ordering of the rest of life when God is at the center gives us the ability to weave together all the bits and pieces of our lives, which often become severely fragmented because of the strains of our surrounding culture. Our various roles and responsibilities have us scurrying in all different directions—taking the kids to soccer practice or ballet class or Boy Scouts, participating in various social-action groups or aerobics, working at several different jobs, trying in the midst of it all to maintain some semblance of home life and family connectedness. Observing the Sabbath each week enables us to establish a deeper sense of family unity. We can establish customs that hold us together and build a special bond of meaningful and Joy-full memories from happy, celebrative times together.

Even those of us who are single can discover such Sabbath wholeness with our friends and extended families. One of my best friends and I have been spending some Sabbaths together since I moved back to Washington. We have tried to be deliberate about the customs we can establish in our friendship to promote greater wholeness. Last Sabbath, in the middle of a quiet afternoon by the fireplace, we decided to make music a more intentional part of our Sabbath times together. Myron immediately went to the piano and played for me two Scott Joplin pieces that were new to his repertoire. Next Sunday, which is the first day of Advent, we will put up the manger scene and angels in my living room and prepare Advent wreaths for both of our homes.

I have found that observing some of my Sabbath customs wherever I travel for speaking engagements brings more wholeness into the fragmented existence of my free-lancing. Since there is continuity in my life from Sabbath to Sabbath (which is the climax of each week), to keep the Sabbath in various homes around the country ties all those places together and helps me to feel at home wherever I am. On all of my teaching trips, I carry two candles, a special wooden "candlestick" given to me by a special friend, and a tiny glass angel, and I especially enjoy sharing the closing prayer at the end of Sabbath day with new friends in new places. That way I can thank God in their presence for them and for the new Sabbath experiences they have offered me.

The Sabbath rhythm, then, enables us to integrate all the scattered parts of our selves into a whole. Even in the times of darkness and sadness, keeping the Sabbath gives us a means for finding wholeness in the midst of our pain. This is illustrated by the unusual ending of 2 Chronicles. After his description of the destruction of the Temple and the city of Jerusalem, of the Babylonian captivity and of the exile, the Chronicler states that the land "enjoyed its Sabbath rests; all the time of its desolation it rested" (2 Chron. 36:21). That ironic assertion probably means that finally, after the Israelites were deported, the land was allowed to rest as God had ordained in Leviticus—that every seven years it should be allowed to remain fallow. (Contemporary farmers certainly have learned the necessity of letting the land rest regularly.) However, I think the statement also implies something beyond a criticism of the Israelites for their failure to observe God's instruction for the Sabbath years' rest for the land. The structure of the text suggests a deeper meaning.

Right after the statement about the land enjoying its Sabbath rest, the text continues with this proclamation of Cyrus, king of Persia, which allowed the Israelites to return to Jerusalem and to rebuild the Temple:

> The LORD, the God of heaven, has given me all the kingdoms of the earth and he has appointed me to build a temple for him at Jerusalem in Judah. Anyone of his people among you—may the LORD his God be with him, and let him go up. (2 Chron. 36:23)

On that positive note, the book ends—after most of 2 Chronicles has been filled with very negative accounts of the failures of the kings of both Israel and Judah to follow the ways of Yahweh.

This incredibly hopeful declaration, in sharp contrast to most of the rest of the book, suggests that when the Chronicler says that "the land enjoyed its Sabbath rests; all the time of its desolation it rested," he also means that Yahweh was very much present during that time. Since observing the Sabbath implies a sense of the presence of Yahweh and since Israel is indicted for its failure to observe the Sabbath and to keep it holy, the point seems to be that, in the absence of the people who failed, the land nevertheless continued to experience God's presence. Yahweh was still at work on behalf of the Israelites, and so, after the seventy years of their exile were completed, he called them back to their homeland. Since they considered the land very much a part of themselves, God's care for the land was understood as an aspect of his faithful love for his people.

Even in the darkest times of my own experience, too, when it seems that God is more absent than present, keeping the Sabbath has given a wholeness to my life that is not otherwise possible. Of course, the pain does not automatically go away. But when the habit of observing the Sabbath is a constant one, the very order of that remembrance enables us to grasp a sense of the presence of Yahweh, who ordained such a keeping of the day. Also, the very practice of the habit provides a means for setting aside the worries and anxieties that attend our dark times. (Remember our discussion in Chapter 3 on ceasing to worry.)

Sometimes our physical or emotional suffering is augmented by the fact that our security has been shattered. Handicaps are not the only things that steal our security; when we pray about them and God doesn't answer our prayers the way we think he should, it shatters the illusory security that comes from our assumption that we know God. Sabbath keeping helps us to discover new dimensions of God, for in its silences we often meet the God hidden in our afflictions. In its disciplines we can learn how pain can be redeemed. Even though God might be silent, our ceasing from spiritual endeavor and our spiritual resting enable us to meet him in the holiness and eternity which the day shares with him.

I am not saying that we will be happy. However, the Scriptures constantly promise us that we will learn new hope and peace—and Joy.[5]

The fact that Sabbath keeping gives us Joy even in our pain is well illustrated by two of Monet's paintings of a haystack in a field. In one of them he demonstrates his uncanny ability to cause that simple subject to glow even though the painting captures it on an overcast day. He makes the haystack beautiful even though it is not colorful in the gloomy darkness—even as the glow of Sabbath intimacy with God brings beauty to our lives even when they are dark with suffering.

On another canvas, the snowy background is very blurry, but still it stands out because of Monet's gift for rendering an unusual quality of light. Similarly, when in our Sabbath embracing we focus on God, who is the Light, his presence enlightens all the paradoxes and puzzles in our lives. We can experience wholeness even though many details of our lives are blurred.

Even as we cease working although our work is not done and spend the Sabbath as if we have no work to do, just so we embrace wholeness on that day even when we are not experiencing wholeness in our present circumstances. The God who ordained that the Sabbath be kept holy is able to watch over our dark nights of the soul and give us Sabbath rest and hope even in the midst of the desolations.

We move from the negative action of trying to cease being anxious into the positive hope of wholeness. As Paul says to the Philippians, not only will "the *peace of God*, which transcends all understanding, guard your hearts and your minds in Christ Jesus," but also "the *God of peace* will be with you" (Phil. 4:7 and 9b, my emphasis). Sabbath keeping ushers us into the wholeness of God's order, the *shalom* of his love.

---

5. See Chapter 12, "Joy When Nothing Seems to Be Good," in my book entitled *I'm Lonely, Lord—How Long? The Psalms for Today* (San Francisco: Harper & Row, 1983).

21. Embracing the World

TO KEEP THE SABBATH means that we embrace a wholly different set of values from those of the world around us. In the first place, we embrace intentionality: we choose carefully how and why we do what we do. We live deliberately in order to embrace a quality of life that is possible only in relationship with the Lord of the Sabbath.

Second, we embrace the values of the Christian community. We spend time together with others of God's people so that the virtues of Christian character can be nourished in our own lives. We want our children to be nurtured in Christ-like qualities so that they will gladly and freely choose to participate in the community of his people.

We embrace time instead of space, people instead of things, holy happenings in history instead of fate, freedom instead of a schedule. We do not *have* to do anything on the Sabbath day, so we are free to move as the Holy Spirit leads us, to participate in whatever opportunities the day gives. Thereby we are set free to care more deeply about others and to discover more richly who they are as fellow children of God.

In addition, we embrace giving instead of requiring. The

145

Sabbath is a day for sharing, for gifting others in many ways, for knowing that the Lord of the Sabbath provides abundantly for us so that we can, in turn, be generous.

The Sabbath day often enables us to discover new insights into our own calling in life and to embrace that calling more thoroughly. This equips us for living out the truth of God's presence in our lives throughout the week in new ways.

Finally, embracing all of these values leads to greater wholeness. To keep the Sabbath is closely connected with God's *shalom*, for we can experience the wholeness of his design only if we follow the orderly pattern—commanded in his Word and written into our being—for six days of work and a day of rest.

Sabbath keeping is often disparaged as not useful, but we certainly do serve the world better out of the wholeness, order, revived spirits, empowered emotions, healthy bodies, renewed minds, authentic relationships, and nurtured senses of ourselves that Sabbath keeping creates. We are much more able to be healers in this sin-sick world when we ourselves have experienced the profound healing that is made possible when we keep the Sabbath. Furthermore, our Sabbath reflection and worship make more urgent our desire to reflect the character of our God, who cares about the poor, feeds the hungry, delivers the oppressed, and brings peace to the world.

As a result, Sabbath keeping changes the world. The practice does not remove us from the world—as some sort of oddballs who retreat every seven days into our own private "religious" sphere. Rather, it plunges us more deeply into the world and its needs because it carries us more deeply into the heart and purposes of God.

We learn this especially from Jesus. Time after time the Gospel narratives state that he was teaching on the Sabbath or healing on the Sabbath, as was his custom. Yet he observed the Sabbath and sanctified it as a holy day. Nowhere in the Gospels do we read that he worked. Furthermore, we can tell from the obedience of his followers—who rested on the Sabbath day and did not go to his tomb to anoint his body more thoroughly for its burial—that he had not instructed them in any way other than to observe the Sabbath day. (See, for example, Luke 23:56b.) Jesus did not negate the Sabbath command of the Hebrew Scriptures.

We do not, therefore, spend the Sabbath trying to save the world. As we saw in the chapters about resting in Section II, our observation of the day equips and empowers us physically, spiritually, emotionally, intellectually, financially, and socially—that is, wholly—to minister to the world on the other six days of the week.

We will not, of course, neglect opportunities should they arise. The Sabbath was made for us, after all, and not we for it. When Jesus met a woman bent over double (Luke 13:10-17) or a man with dropsy (Luke 14:1-6), he gladly cared for those individuals, even though it was the Sabbath. Similarly, we don't want to be so rigid about our Sabbath that we don't offer to help when there is a need—for example, to change someone's flat tire or to help with dishes at camp on Sunday. In general, however, we will embrace the world on Sabbath days by refraining from trying to fix it.

Instead, we will realize that our very keeping of the Sabbath gives testimony to the efficacy of God's provision in our lives and witness to our trust for the future in his goodness. Out of the wholeness that Sabbath keeping creates, we will call the world to new wholeness.

Sabbath keeping is the very thing that our technological world needs. Instead of society's criterion of efficiency, keeping the Sabbath offers the will and purposes of God as the ultimate criteria. Instead of technological sterility and control, Sabbath keeping offers the gift of intimacy in the Christian community and the freedom of a relationship with a faithful covenant God whose control bequeaths to us perfect *shalom*.

PART IV
FEASTING

Rejoice in the Lord always. I will say it again: Rejoice!

—Philippians 4:4

Celebration is the honoring of that which we hold most dear. Celebration is delighting in that which tells us who we are. Celebration is taking the time to cherish each other. Celebration is returning with open arms and thankful hearts to our Maker.

—Sara Wenger Shenk,
Why Not Celebrate!

FTER THE CEASING, the resting, and the embracing comes the feasting. Observing the Sabbath includes not only the freedom from, and repentance for, work and worry (ceasing), the renewing of our whole being in grace-based faith (resting), and the intentionality of our choosing and valuing (embracing), but also the fun and festivity of a weekly eschatological party. I use the word *eschatological* to emphasize our experience of both present Joy in our feasting and anticipation of the future, eternal consummation of Joy.

Sabbath celebration is especially needed in our technological society. In the first place, feasting is a right-brained activity that gives us a better balance—since most of us spend our workdays engaged primarily in left-brained activities. Our Sabbath activities make more use of our senses, our emotions, our creativity, our intuitions.

Furthermore, the intimacy of genuine feasting is not a false intimacy. Most contemporary "parties" create the illusion of intimacy through the influence of alcohol or through the deceptions of social manipulations. The party that we enjoy in our Sabbath keeping is a celebration of true love, initiated by the Creator of the Sabbath and imitated by those of us who know him as Lord of our lives and who welcome Queen Sabbath into our lives.

Accordingly, in this section we will first explore the eternal dimension of our feasting. Then we will consider music, beauty, food, and affection as resources for our celebrations. Finally, we will contemplate the paradoxes of festivity and the intertwining of all the aspects of our Sabbath keeping.

22. *Feasting on the Eternal*

ONE OF THE MOST FRUSTRATING THINGS about our contemporary festivals is that they are over so soon and the feasting abruptly comes to an end. Last week, after all my preparations for Thanksgiving—making pumpkin chiffon pies, preparing dressing and stuffing a turkey, setting the table with my grandmother's china and with flowers and pretty napkins—the feast with several friends was over far too quickly.

Sabbath keeping teaches the dialectical truth that Christian feasting is both temporal and eternal. Our weekly celebrations help us to be more aware that God is eternally present, but the fact that Sunday moves on into Monday keeps reminding us that our short-lived Sabbath celebrations are but a foretaste of the eternal feast that we will someday enjoy in God's presence.

Consequently, one of the aspects of our Sabbath keeping is an emphasis on its ephemerality. At the end of the day, when the candles are lit for the Havdalah prayers, we bid the Sabbath good-bye with a great longing in our hearts. We enjoyed the presence of the queen and long for her return. We have

153

tasted the delights of the day and long for their eternal fulfillment.

A larger aspect of our Sabbath keeping, however, is the
recognition that through this practice we can find God and touch
the eternal in a way otherwise not possible. Abraham Heschel
makes this point compellingly:

> For where shall the likeness of God be found? There is no
> quality that space has in common with the essence of God.
> There is not enough freedom on the top of the mountain;
> there is not enough glory in the silence of the sea. Yet the
> likeness of God can be found in time, which is eternity in
> disguise.[1]

The way in which Sabbath keeping makes possible this discovery of the eternal became more clear to me one Sabbath evening when I was feasting on a new book about Monet. I had spent
the afternoon tuning the strings of my Celtic harp for the first
time since my move from Indiana to Washington and musing
about how much I'd forgotten in the months that I had been
traveling to teach and had not been able to practice. Those reflections made me terribly aware of the ephemerality of everything
in life, so the amazing paintings in the book about Monet caught
me up in the wonder of the great artist's ability to capture the
eternal in a moment.

When Monet wanted to capture a certain effect—a particular kind of light on a landscape, for example—he would refuse to
continue painting as soon as the effect changed. Therefore, when
he worked on his well-known series of haystack paintings, he carried several canvasses to the spot he had chosen and waited for
certain effects to appear. He had learned to analyze and record
what he saw with lightning speed, so he could return to the same
spot for many days and continue painting on all of the canvasses
by concentrating on each in turn as the particular effect it was

---

1. Heschel, *The Sabbath: Its Meaning for Modern Man* (New York:
Farrar, Straus & Giroux, 1951), p. 16.

meant to render appeared.[2] In this way Monet could capture eternally—or, more accurately, for at least as long as the paintings and the photographs of them last—the transient moments of those effects. When eight of his haystack paintings were exhibited at the Chicago Art Institute a few years ago, I spent more than half an hour staring at them—overwhelmed by the light he captured, longing to embrace the eternity intimated in those paintings.

Just as Monet went back day after day to capture an effect, so we go back week after week for the effect of the Sabbath in order to paint into our spirits the eternal, the presence of God. We do this primarily through our personal and corporate study of the Scriptures, in moments of silence, and through our personal and corporate worship. Furthermore, the continual repetition of the very habits of Sabbath keeping paints the light of the eternal into our souls and stirs up eager longing for the Sabbath consummation.

The following Jewish folk-tale, which Chaim Grade tells in *My Mother's Sabbath Days,* underscores both the eschatological hope of the Sabbath and the importance of our Sabbath activities of Bible study, worship, and prayer for experiencing the presence of God:

A pious Jew loses his way in a forest late one Friday afternoon. The sun sets and the pious man begins to weep in sorrow, because he will be unable to observe the Sabbath. Suddenly he sees a palace standing amidst the trees. An old man appears and motions wordlessly to the lost Jew to follow him. The old man leads him to a fragrant pool, in which the Jew bathes, and then gives him luxurious raiment to wear in honor of the Sabbath. When the guest tries to ask a question, the old man signals him to be still. Then he leads the wanderer into a chamber that glitters with silver and gold, with pearls and precious stones. From there the guide takes him into a second chamber, where candelabra and chandeliers gleam with the radiance of the seven great lights

---

2. *Monet: A Retrospective,* ed. Charles F. Stuckey (New York: Park Lane, 1985), p. 28.

of the Six Days of Creation. And so the guest wanders, enchanted and bedazzled, from room to room, each more beautifully and splendidly adorned than the one before— until, in the seventh and last chamber, he is approached by seven ancient men who with their white beards resemble a forest of snow-covered oak trees. They welcome him and tell him that with his arrival they now have a minyan [the ten men necessary for a Jewish service to be held]. This bewilders the poor Jew: here are these seven elders, he is the eighth, and the old man accompanying him makes nine, but nowhere does he see the required tenth man. Yet he vividly senses the tenth everywhere about him, like the radiance of the Divine Presence. And he is seized by overwhelming feelings of fear, of awe and reverence, though of the ordinary kind of fear that makes the limbs tremble, there is in his heart not a trace. Now an elder wearing a royal crown takes his place at the cantor's pulpit and welcomes the Sabbath, chanting with such sweetness that one might think him to be the Psalmist himself. After prayers, the Jew is told to wash his hands, and he is then served meat that tastes like the Wild Ox which the righteous will eat in Paradise, and wine with the taste of the wine reserved for the coming of the Messiah. And thus does he spend the entire Sabbath in the elders' company, in prayer, in singing Sabbath hymns, in study of the Torah. And if he essays even a single word about profane matters, they silence him with a gesture. At the conclusion of the Sabbath, he is given spices to smell which have the fragrance of the Tree of Life. Finally, the old man who has been his guide leads him back out into the forest, and whispers in his ear that he has just been in Paradise. And the elders are Abraham, Isaac, and Jacob, Moses and Aaron, and David and Solomon, and he, the caretaker of the palace, is Eliezer, servant to the Patriarch Abraham. And the tenth for the minyan was the Holy One Himself, Blessed be He. . . .[3]

---

3. Grade, *My Mother's Sabbath Days: A Memoir,* trans. Channa Kleinerman Goldstein and Inna Hecker Grade (New York: Alfred A. Knopf, 1986), pp. 337-38.

I especially love that story because as Christians we believe that the Messiah has come, that Jesus Christ is the One for whom we were waiting. In our Sabbath practices we seek God's presence and look forward to the day when Jesus will come again and take us home to celebrate the Sabbath eternally with him. Accordingly, Karen Burton Mains, author of *Making Sunday Special,* emphasizes that our Saturday habit of getting ready for Sunday is the discipline of getting ready for the Lord's final coming.[4]

A major Sabbath activity for both Jews and Christians is our reading and study of the Scriptures—both with others and by ourselves—by which we come to know their diverse portraits of God. Many eternal aspects of his character are revealed by the inspired words of the apostles and the prophets. Although the language and the images are transient, they capture the essence of God and reveal it to those minds and spirits that are open to the continued inspiration of the Holy Spirit. In Karl Barth's terms, the Word of God becomes Revelation to us when we receive it as God's Word addressed personally to each of us.

Since God is eternally the same, we can receive his revelation of himself in the twentieth century even though it was first recorded in the language of the seventh century B.C.E. or the first century C.E. Just as God revealed himself to be compassionate and gracious to the Hebrew people, and just as he revealed himself in a manger and on a cross and by an empty tomb, so he makes himself known to us every time we bow before his Word. It is important to stress that we must stand under his Word in order truly to understand it, for if we open the Scriptures in order to pick them apart or to elevate our own learning above the message proclaimed therein, we will not hear what the Spirit is saying to us. Only with humility and gratitude can we approach the table of God's Word to feast there on his eternal love.

Unfortunately, such a caution has to be issued in this book because the spirit of our times often elevates one's own biblical

---

4. Mains, *Making Sunday Special* (Waco, Tex.: Word Books, 1987), p. 58.

exegetical skills over the biblical witness itself. Having spent many years in theological programs at four different graduate schools, I am frustrated by that kind of superciliousness and think it imperative that the Church be called back to humility before the wisdom of God. I am not at all antagonistic to the use of critical tools; what I object to is an attitude that focuses on human achievement rather than the authority of God.

Sabbath keeping helps us by offering a day in which we recognize that we are incapable of providing for ourselves— either physically or spiritually. If we are to feast spiritually, God must provide the manna of his Word. Only by his grace has he chosen to reveal himself to us; only by his grace can we understand and believe what his revelation declares.

Besides the spoken and heard and read Word of God, we need to recapture in our noisy culture the silence that is also a language of God. With the constant coughing of the mass media in our world, we find it difficult to hear what God is teaching us in the silences. Observing the Sabbath offers us continued practice in keeping silent in order to hear "the yearning [of our spirits for God], the Prayer [he has] planted [within] us, and to allow ourselves to be shaped and moved by it."[5]

I am not writing as a mystic here, for I have never heard God speak audibly out of the clouds of silence. Rather, in the uncluttered space of silence there is room to pay attention to the still small voice of God nudging our consciences or clarifying our thoughts or imprinting his peace into our souls. As the writer of Ecclesiastes says, "Better is a handful of quietness than two hands full of toil and a striving after wind" (4:6, RSV).

Sometimes silence overtakes us on our Sabbath walks as we stand quietly beholding a magnificent view or as we hush our speech to listen to the wind or the buzz of bees or the merry song of a distant meadowlark. Sometimes silence pervades our Bible reading (it is always best to shut off all distracting sounds),

---

5. Leonard Beechy, "Three Levels of Prayer," *Gospel Herald,* 20 Nov. 1984, p. 806.

and the text speaks to us loudly and clearly. Sometimes silence sneaks up on us in the middle of a Sabbath happiness, and suddenly we are aware that we are in the presence of God. Most recently I experienced lovely moments of silence when my friends Linden and Brenda took Myron and me to a park of Northern California redwoods where we solemnly surveyed the magnificence of God in the trees' towering grandeur. A few Sundays later, I sat beside an Iowa lake and quietly gazed over its placid waters at the sun-bright colors of fall leaves. Their passing show in contrast to the seeming eternity of the lake put my fragile human existence in proper perspective in relation to God.

Many times we cannot hear God's voice because we want him to speak our language. Only when we love him so much that we prefer his ways to ours will we be open to receive his gracious revelation of himself.

God's will is the way of holiness. The Beatitudes promise us that those who are pure in heart shall see God (Matt. 5:8). That is an immense promise that transforms our lifestyles. We choose to be pure not because of guilt over our failures or fear of the consequences, but because we desire to see God and to know his presence more intimately in all the moments of our days. The great gift of Sabbath keeping is that we set aside a whole day to focus on seeing God, to choose his holy ways in order to experience his presence.

Both in the silences of solitude and in the true fellowship of community, God becomes more real to us. Worship is made up of the paradoxical combinations of both solitude and community and of both silence and speech or song (although most worshiping communities are not very good at observing long moments of silence).

The corporate worship in which we engage on the Sabbath day is the main event that puts us in touch with the eternal essence of God. Unfortunately, our common expression "I'm going to church" often destroys our sense that we are "going to worship." To say the latter might remind us that worship is a feast, a delightful experience, a holy time in the presence of God.

Even as we must stand under the Scriptures in order to understand them, so the attitudes and actions necessary for worship let God be the subject. We wait expectantly for his revelation of himself rather than try to manipulate him or put on a show or fulfill an obligation. We do not go to church; we enter into a worship experience. The order of worship is not worship; it makes space and time for worship to happen—but if we continue to remain the subject (focusing on *our* actions of worship), then true worship never materializes. The difference between thinking and worship is that in the latter, God is the subject. Through the liturgy or the Word or the community, he invades. To adore God, to bow before him, and to await his revelation cause us to focus on his character and meditate on his presence to the point that we lose track of ourselves and what we are doing in the sublime mystery of receiving his gracious gift of himself.

Certain things contribute to our receptivity, and for each of us those things differ. For some reason, trumpets have always stirred me to a deeper awareness of the majesty of God. That probably goes back to my childhood, when my father would arrange brass accompaniments or descants for the Easter hymns. Similarly, processions of banners often stir me to recognize the presence of God, but whenever those processions become personally showy or include some disrespectful participants, the whole effect of the sublime stateliness is spoiled for me.

Recognizing these factors leads me to posit certain criteria against which we can measure the value and appropriateness of the things we do in worship. The first major requirement is reverence. This is often missing in contemporary worship services in which Christ is known too much as a good buddy. There is a great need for awe when we stand in the presence of God.

Perhaps even our attire contributes to whether or not we experience that awe. When I was a little girl and my family was less than rich, I always had one special dress for Sundays. I was never allowed to wear it on any other day, and it had to last until the next Christmas or Easter, when I would receive a new special dress for worship days. I do not at all regret that we didn't have much money in those times, because otherwise I might never have learned this important lesson: that one dresses with particular care on Sundays—not to show off one's finery before others, but to be duly respectful before God and to honor him.[6] I remember that even as a small child I had a deep sense of the holiness of the Sabbath day because I anticipated wearing my Sunday dress. It was very important to make Saturday-night preparations in order to look my best the following day to honor God.

In the sanctuary on Sunday mornings, too, there was a deep sense of the presence of God. Even when I was very little, I knew that my usually boisterous outside-play noises (to be distinguished from the exuberance and Joy of worship) did not belong in this holy place. I long for such a reverence to be restored in contemporary worship.

Of course, I recognize that such reverence too easily degenerates into stilted, stuffy silence and frozen rigidity. Certainly the casualness of contemporary forms was intended to offset the lack of personalness that develops when reverence is overdone. However, it seems to me that the pendulum has swung too far in the other direction and that we need to move back into the center. If the dialectical poles of reverence for God and familiarity with God could be held in better tension, we might be able to appreciate more fully both his transcendent and his intimate presence in our worship experiences. God is King of kings and Lord of lords as well as Gentle Shepherd.

Another set of dialectical poles that must be held together in balance is the contrasting pair of tradition and newness. In our worship the traditions give us narrative reminders of our history and heritage as the people of God. On the other hand, lest our

---

6. In *Life Is with People: The Culture of the Shtetl* (New York: Schocken Books, 1952), Mark Zborowski and Elizabeth Herzog describe in detail the Jewish attention to dress on the Sabbath. In the Eastern European shtetl (small village) even the poorest male Jews would own the white-wool talis koton with its knotted fringes, the black "silk" Sabbath caftan, and the black cap. Women wore black silk dresses and their best jewelry, especially necklaces of pearls (pp. 40-42).

worship become empty ritual, we make room in our Sabbath assemblies for spontaneity, the freshness of the moment's sense of
grace, a sharing of the things that God is presently doing in our
lives. Our traditional liturgies must continue to call us anew to
the funeral worship of dying to ourselves, to the holiday worship
of celebrating all our gifts, to the wedding worship of meeting
the Sabbath Bride (for whose coming we carefully prepare our
orders of worship). Just as a marriage takes continued work, so
it takes special commitment to preserve worship time and meaning. Thus, we celebrate our memories in the traditions and our
present Joy in the Sabbath exhilaration and exaltation that differ
from what we experience on ordinary days.

Another important criterion for worship is whether or not
it proclaims truth. Is the message of the preacher in accord with
the truth of the Scriptures, or does it merely expound his or her
personal opinions? Are the selections of music appropriately
truthful? That is, does the music match the words? Is the music
aesthetically congruent? (More will be said about music in the
next chapter.) Does the worship service enable us to step out of
the world in order to assess it more objectively, to see things as
they really are? Does our worship promote the awareness that
all truth is to be found in God and that everything else must be
discerned carefully against the standard of his truth?

Other criteria include whether or not our worship express-
es beauty and goodness.[7] Are our souls uplifted by the revelation of God's character in the beauty of our surroundings and
auditory experiences? Does the behavior of the pastor match his
or her words? Does our behavior as a congregation match our
words? Do our actions as believers convey God's goodness in
daily life so that our worship is not hypocritical? In other words,
does our Sabbath continue to inform the rest of our week? Is our
Sunday worship incarnated in the worship of our daily work?

---

7. I am grateful to my former editor, Roy M. Carlisle, for helping
me to learn that true worship pursues the philosophical goals of truth,
beauty, and goodness.

Related to these issues is another set of dialectical poles—that of objectivity and subjectivity. In our worship we need the narrative reminders of God's interventions on behalf of his people and the proclamation of his promises for our lives. On the other hand, there are many things about God that cannot be asserted. We lack the vocabulary to express the deep things of God, so we must let them simply soak into our beings through means other than words. Sabbath worship, therefore, must also include rituals, images, symbols, sounds, textures, tastes, and fragrances that evoke adoration of the heart beyond rationalizations of the mind. In their overly objective analysis of the technique in paintings, critics sometimes miss the overall effect of the art they are examining. Similarly, theologians especially need Sabbath worship to avoid scientific religiosity and to experience being enveloped in the embrace of God. Furthermore, even though books or photographs or memories help us experience works of art, they can't capture the total effect of the works themselves. Similarly, our tools of worship are not ends in themselves, but are meant to enable us to enjoy the real thing—the presence of God himself.

A final criterion is whether or not worship is cohesive with the rest of life. Worship that enables us, on the one hand, to touch the eternal is closely connected, on the other hand, with the rest of life, with the daily nitty-gritty of the workweek. Wholistic worship involves all the aspects of our lives in the meaning of the Sabbath. Moreover, worship enables us to experience the inward and outward movement of coming together to feast in the presence of God and then going out to carry his presence into the rest of the world. In order to function as such a bridge, our worship includes prayers for the members of the community and for the needs of the world, Scripture lessons that provide the narrative which nurtures the formation of our character for daily living, sermons that instruct us in the ways of God's kingdom so that we can extend that kingdom every day, offerings that are gathered to support the church's ministry in the world, relationships that support us in our personal ministries throughout the week, and liturgy and hymns that remind us of the power of God at work in us in our daily vocations.

In the same way, all the other customs of Sabbath keeping put us in touch with the eternal and yet connect us to daily life. We set apart this day and its meals and activities in order that the meals and activities of the rest of the week might partake of the holiness of this day. To keep the Sabbath enables us to become more and more a Sabbath people, and that characterization affects the way we relate to everything else in our lives. As we have often noted in this book, the Sabbath is the climax of the week, and everything else derives its character from our keeping of that day. As Abraham Heschel declares, "What we *are* depends on what *the Sabbath is* to us."[8]

Sabbath keeping is not a dry duty or an oppressive obligation. It is a delight, a feasting on that which is eternal rather than a scrambling after the ephemeral success, the amassed wealth, the ceaseless activities, the elegant refinement that Americans think will grant them permanent happiness. Instead of trying to create our own security, we worship the one who *is* our security. The presence of God in our worship, in his Word, and in our customs for keeping the day transforms us for the entire week into persons whose values are not transient, into Sabbath people who carry the kingdom of God within them wherever they go.

Because God's eternity enfolds us in our Sabbath celebrations, our weekday lives become more ordered by his priorities. Rather than chasing after fleeting, self-centered goals, we will want to invest ourselves in God's purposes in the world. We will delight in becoming agents for his purposes of caring for the poor, delivering the oppressed, announcing the good news of salvation, building peace in the world—not with any false idealism that we can bring the kingdom of God to its culmination in this world, but with the sure hope that God is always at work to create peace and justice and freedom and that we can participate in his eternal purposes because of the Holy Spirit's

---

8. Heschel, *The Sabbath,* p. 89, emphases his.

power within and through us. We also look forward to the day when God's kingdom will come in all its fullness and our once-a-week Sabbaths will be transformed into an eternal Sabbath feast in God's perfect presence.

23. Feasting with Music

IN THE ORIGINAL PLAN of this book I had not intended to devote an entire chapter to music in worship; I thought that subject could be included in the concept of feasting on beauty in our Sabbath keeping since music is only one aspect of the auditory dimension of the larger whole of beauty. However, that plan was changed by a disturbing experience I had this past weekend.

I was invited to teach a module on "rock music" for a Lutheran youth convention. I knew that a large number of high-school students would attend this session, so I wanted to find a way to discuss the subject without immediately polarizing the audience into those who detest rock music and think it is of the devil (many of the adults who would be present) and those who love rock music and are angry at adults for rejecting it (most of the teenagers who would be present).

I thought it would be fruitful to place the subject within a larger framework by discussing the issue in terms of general criteria for discerning what is and isn't helpful for nurturing a certain kind of character. Since we could assume that most of those present really did desire to live godly lives, perhaps we could work together to consider the kinds of values that we want to hold and live by as we seek to be followers of Christ.

I began the class by proposing that Christian ethics is not a system of rules. To legislate that rock music is not permitted only makes youth all the more eager to listen to it. Besides, simply making rules does not help anyone do a better job of thinking. On the other hand, a teleological approach to ethics[1] does not really work because no one can know what will be the result of listening to certain kinds of music. We can suggest that violent and sexist music promotes crime and treating women as objects, but we cannot know specifically what other factors contribute to certain outcomes and behaviors.

Therefore, it seems to me that to consider the question of what kind of people we are becoming is the best way to approach ethical matters. When we ask what kind of people we want to be, that question must be followed by the realization that a certain milieu promotes a certain kind of character. If we are the people of God, our milieu is the Christian community, and within that framework our growth in Christian character is nourished.

I told the youth that I am not opposed to rock music. Some of it is very good—both in its message and in the skill of its performers. But other kinds of rock music inculcate values that I find objectionable. (The same could be said for advertisements, which are often designed to stir up erotic feelings or to encourage materialism.) I asked the youth what kind of people they wanted to become and what kinds of music would nurture such a character.

What shocked me was that several of the high-school students present rejected the whole notion that our milieu greatly influences (although sometimes very subtly) our character. They insisted that their values were not affected when they listened to

---

1. Teleology emphasizes the end result of behavior. The most prevalent form of this sort of ethical thinking is utilitarianism. Teleological ethics can lead to the idea that a certain end justifies the means, whereas deontological ethics (the ethics of rules) emphasizes the means whereby an end is reached.

certain rock songs that promote sexism, violence, or drugs. They just liked the beat or the melody or thought the performer was cute or handsome or whatever.

Their reaction was very disturbing to me. It demonstrated that to a great extent the Christian Church has become so enculturated that we don't realize we are enculturated. We have become so used to a polluted milieu that we don't realize the damage it is doing to us. Later I commented on my fear to an acquaintance, and he responded that when he was in high school he didn't think that the music he listened to was affecting his values, either. However, now when he looks back on the subsequent events in his life, he realizes that some of his sexual behavior was the negative result of the subtle way in which the milieu had influenced his character.

This whole event made me realize how imperative it is that the Christian community take more seriously its responsibility to provide a positive, godly milieu in which youth can learn the values of that community. Properly translated, 2 Corinthians 5:17 declares, "If anyone is in Christ, *there is* a whole new creation." When we become Christians, our whole milieu is different!

This lengthy preface to the chapter is not intended to suggest that the Church should be totally opposed to rock music. Many modern songs nurture Christian character more effectively than some of our hymns! What I do want to stress is that the members of the Church, of all people, should be the ones most devoted to the criterion that *all* their music should promote godly values. Specifically, the music of the worship service should be appropriately conducive to worship.

Does the music in your congregation nurture a healthy sense of sexuality in all members? Some of our hymns are exclusive; a few of them picture Jesus as some sort of wimp; some of them promote a lopsided view of the ministry of each person within the community of believers.

Does the music in your congregation promote violence? More and more I am troubled by such hymns as "Onward, Chris-

tian Soldiers, Marching as to War."[2] Such hymns sometimes foster
the kind of attitudes that led to the Crusades.

Does the music in your congregation elevate God alone?
Or is it so subjectively slanted that it focuses on me, the wor-
shiper, and my feelings?

What kind of philosophy of life does your congregational
music promote? Is God the center of our existence and thereby
the focus for everything else, or do our songs promote bad theology, an inward-turned philosophy of life?

Of course, one of the main questions that must be asked is
the question of aesthetics, and in this dimension much of modern
Christian music is objectionable. At the closing worship service
of the youth convention I previously described, a folk-singing
group sang a version of the Lord's Prayer in which the music did
not at all fit the meaning of the words. One young girl a few rows
in front of me was cutting her fingernails during the song. I'm
sure that if she had realized it was the Lord's Prayer, she wouldn't
have been so sacrilegious—at least, I hope she would not have
been—but the music did not lend itself to any sort of reverence,
nor did it sound like the earnest petitions of the people of God
addressed to their caring Father.

Aesthetics involves the combination of beauty, order, diversity, and congruity.[3] Of course, beauty takes many different forms

---

2. An obviously thoughtful youth at the convention asked me, in
response to my objection to that hymn, how I dealt with the whole subject of Holy War in the Old Testament. That is a very good question
which requires an entire book to answer thoroughly, but briefly I must
assert that Holy War is actually a kind of peacemaking. It must be properly understood within the framework of the way in which God was leading the people of Israel away from the violence of the culture that surrounded them. If we took seriously the edict to burn all the booty so
that war could not be fought for personal aggrandizement, it might
change the prevalence of war in our society. An excellent but easy-to-
understand guide on this subject is Lois Barrett's *The Way God Fights:
War and Peace in the Old Testament* (Scottdale, Penn.: Herald Press, 1987).

3. Indeed, a growing number of people are concerned about aesthetics in worship. Even Ann Landers' column on 16 Nov. 1987 was

and is manifested by a great variety of tools. Such aspects as the loveliness of melody, the skill of performance, harmonic texturing, instrumental coloring, contrapuntal development, and so forth all contribute to the beauty of music.

Much of our music is orderly, but it might also be boring. I remember, for example, the endless folk masses that sang very superficial lines to the constantly repeated melody of "Michael, Row the Boat Ashore." No wonder youth cannot stand the music of our worship services. So much of the stuff created in the attempt to capture their interest is so trite that they can't help but recognize its shallowness.

On the other hand, some music that has diversity is also too chaotic. The important criterion is congruence between the music and its message. If we are portraying the chaos of evil, then the music should be appropriately disorderly. If we are talking about the majesty of God, then the hymn must be sung at a majestic tempo and neither dragged nor rushed.

That comment leads to a consideration of how hymns should be sung. Two very dear friends of mine, Janet and Kent Hill, have awakened me to both the challenge and the delight of singing hymns. They remind me every time I am with them that one must sing the entire phrase and not breathe in the middle of a line. That seems such a simple thing, but it utterly changes the way we sing hymns if we pay attention to it. When I worked with the Hills for a week at a camp last summer, their daily periods of hymn singing exposed all my bad habits again. Consequently, during the following week when I was serving a different camp, I paid more attention to the way we were singing and was horrified by the way we chopped up lines and destroyed the message.

A very well-known stewardship hymn illustrates the point well. What happens to us spiritually if we sing, "Take my life and let it be [breath] Consecrated, Lord, to Thee"? Unfortunately, that

---

filled with many letters expressing disapproval over many things that happen in contemporary worship.

is the way the line is usually sung, because the rhythm of the music promotes taking a breath in the middle of the phrase. Only if we consciously pray "Take my life and let it *be consecrated,* Lord, to Thee" can that music communicate to us the commitment for which we are longing.

I do not want this chapter to be entirely negative. It seems to me, however, that stern warnings about the destructiveness of much of our music must be issued to challenge the Church to be more faithful to its privilege of worship. If we could sing hymns well and search for music that is appropriate to what we are trying to do in worship and the values we want to inculcate, our music could be a veritable feast.

Last Thursday on Thanksgiving the congregation in which I participate offered a musical feast that was wonderfully inspiring. I had been up since six that morning to prepare for dinner, so I went to worship at ten feeling tired and a little out of sorts. (I'm obviously *not* a morning person!) However, I was soon lifted from my lethargy by the Joy that was shining in the faces of the members of the choir. One could easily tell that they loved what they were doing as they sang praises to God. The choir director led them to hold together the entire phrase "Take my life and let it be consecrated." She used trumpeters, a bell choir, and organ with piano, and thus involved many members of the congregation in the worship experience. In addition, the children of the Sunday school sang two special anthems. All the music was appropriate to its message, and the resources of the congregation were used thoroughly.

When I complimented the choir director afterward and thanked her for the sheer delight of hearing such good music, she reminded me that on most Sundays it is not possible to pull out all the stops like that. I was grateful for her reminder, but added that it wasn't the immensity of the production that had impressed me. It was her faithfulness to the message. She had led her choir in expressing what the day meant, and it was obvious that they had enjoyed that expression under her leadership.

No matter how small a congregation is or how untalented

its musicians might be, the music of worship can be a feast. What matters is the state of the heart and that what is done is appropriate to the message of faith. I would rather hear a few mistakes from students who play from their hearts for the glory of God than all the right notes from a professional choir that has no soul. Ephesians 5:19 encourages us to sing and make music to the Lord in our hearts (whether or not we have great vocal chords!), and many of the Psalms urge us to make a Joy-full noise to the Lord and to shout to God with cries of Joy. However, we must also encourage each student to play music appropriate to his or her level of skill.

It probably is obvious from my comments that I vastly prefer classical music to rock, but I want very much to be open to accept whatever worship music fits the criteria outlined here. I have been equally moved by Bach and Gaither, White Heart and Wesley. What matters is how the Holy Spirit is using their music to mold who I am—who we are—becoming.

24. Feasting with Beauty

ONE OF THE REASONS that I am so attracted to the Jewish observance of the Sabbath day is that throughout the history of Judaica there has been an emphasis on the beauty of the day—especially in the concept of Queen Sabbath, for whom the house is made ready and all things are intended to be lovely. In a society such as ours, scarred by hatred and violence, there is a tremendous need for great intentionality concerning beauty.

The Jewish liturgy for Sabbath eve includes the lovely hymn "Lechah Dodi" ("Come, My Beloved"), composed by Solomon Alkabetz in Salonika, Turkey, in the 1500s to welcome the beautiful Sabbath Queen.[1] The hymn also charges humankind to administer the creation in a godly manner. Other table hymns, called Zemirot, used for Jewish family times of worship, focus on the desire of every creature to praise the Creator. The Sabbath itself encourages God's people to discover the secrets of the creation

---

1. Philip S. Berg, *Kabbalah for the Layman: A Guide to Cosmic Consciousness, An Opening to the Portals of Jewish Mysticism* (The Old City Jerusalem: Press of the Research Centre of Kabbalah, 1981), pp. 181-83.

and especially to refrain from even the smallest work which would deny that God is the Creator and Master of the world. By observing a day of holiness and refraining from activity, we imitate the Creator and enter into his Sabbath rest.[2]

When we Christians rest as if all our work were done, we celebrate God's creative and redemptive accomplishments on our behalf. Knowing that God is the perfect Creator, we spend the day delighting in the beauties of his creation and thereby growing in our love for the Master Designer and Craftsman.

Observing the Sabbath gives us the opportunity to be as careful as we can to fill our lives with beauty and to share beauty with the world around us. When we observe a day especially set apart for beauty, all the rest of life is made more beautiful. That truth is illustrated by Monet's painting entitled "Spring through the Blossoms." The canvas is entirely filled with white-flowered trees except for one bright-red roof in the center of the composition. Our eyes are immediately drawn to that roof, and its brilliance makes us more aware of the loveliness of the trees. In the same way, focusing on beauty on one day causes us to notice it on the other six days of the week. The Sabbath becomes a garden park in the midst of the technicization of life; it brings us tranquility and intimacy, sensitivity and creativity, butterflies and goldfinches and roses!

Some dimensions of beauty specifically relate to our worship life, including the beauty of our sanctuaries and the beauty of our homes as temples. How our places of worship are designed and decorated makes a great difference in our Sabbath attitudes. Just recently Professor Ernst Schwidder, an artist addressing the subject of architecture and liturgy, said, "First you design a building, and then the building designs you." We want to design our places of worship to be congruent with what we are doing in them and to continue to instruct us as we gather there.

I am grateful for my heritage in the Lutheran Church be-

---

2. B. S. Jacobson, *The Sabbath Service: An Exposition and Analysis of Its Structure, Contents, Language, and Ideas,* trans. Leonard Oschry (Tel Aviv: "Sinai" Publishing, 5741/1981).

cause it nurtured me in an atmosphere of symbols. Even when I did not understand anything of the sermons, I did learn from the statues and stained-glass windows depicting Jesus, from the altar carvings and paraments in the sanctuary of my childhood.

The importance of symbols in my worship life struck home for me fiercely the first Sunday that I was away at college. In the sanctuary of St. Paul's Lutheran Church in Napoleon, Ohio, my hometown congregation, the front of the nave is dominated by two large stained-glass windows depicting the hand of blessing of the Father, a figure of Christ, and a dove representing the Holy Spirit. Each Sunday as we confessed our faith in the words of the Apostles' or the Nicene Creed, I contemplated the images of the three Persons of the Trinity in that pair of windows and affirmed my belief in God. On my first Sunday away from home, at that point in the liturgy, my head spontaneously lifted and my eyes searched for the symbols. With a great gasp I realized that the front wall was empty, and it took me awhile to recover my equilibrium enough to speak the words of the creed. The stained-glass windows of my home church were very useful tools for nurturing my faith. Their beauty lifted me in awe to contemplate the mystery of the Trinity.

Whatever our liturgical traditions—or absence of them—it is important that our places of worship be places of beauty, and it is especially wonderful if the beauty can be produced by members of the worshiping body. Then the building tells its own special narrative in terms of the people who gather there. When the works of art, the banners, or other furnishings reflect the loving hands of community members, the beauty of these things reinforces the understanding that we are all important ministers in the Church according to our respective gifts. If the labor of another member's workweek adds to the delight of worship on the Sabbath day, the rest of us learn more thoroughly to consecrate all of our weekday labor to the glory of God.

That same understanding carries over into our homes and the importance of beauty there. Especially on the Sabbath day (but throughout the week, too, of course), we want our homes to reflect our care and concern that the home be a place of rest, of fulfillment, of God's gracious love. As we prepare for the Sabbath, we want to make an extra effort for all things to be lovely as a reflection of our honor of the Sabbath Queen, who comes to bless us with her presence. I always try (although I confess I am not always successful) to make room in my Saturday schedule to prepare as much as possible for Queen Sabbath.

The year that I turned twenty, my brother Glen gave me a lovely music box for my birthday. "You are no longer a child and not yet an adult," he wrote, "so let's just celebrate this that we share: The love of beauty and the Joy of music." His gift is like a miniature Bavarian house, with flower boxes at the windows, and, inside, a charming little dancer spins around as the song plays. Several years later, Glen found a piano-shaped music box at a garage sale. He knew I would enjoy it even though its legs were missing—and my friend Myron made for it some beautifully fluted wooden legs. Sometimes on Sabbath days I like to take extra time to play my music boxes and to notice their beauty, which, on busy days, I often pass by without seeing. The conscious enjoyment of loveliness enables me to experience more richly my apartment as a place of God's presence.

Besides making our homes temples of worship, holy places of beauty, we can also enjoy other places of beauty that inspire worship—both in large and small ways. Many Sabbath days offer time for escape into the beauties of literature. Stories of good characters inspire us to be more virtuous, motivate good behavior, and inculcate values. An artist friend taught me to savor especially the illustrations in children's books.

As often as possible I enjoy letting art lift me into the realm of the sublimely beautiful. Trips to museums or time spent perusing a book about a favorite artist are especially uplifting activities for the Sabbath. Some of my books—those that show various images of Christ, the religious paintings of Rembrandt, or artistic treasures from European museums and cathedrals that I've visited—carry me into an atmosphere of worship.

I must emphasize that our moments of beauty need not be

major to change the whole timbre of the day. Yesterday, a Sabbath Sunday, I was returning from a speaking engagement and had to pass through the San Francisco airport. I had been there a month before and had discovered in one of the quieter waiting areas some gorgeous flat-weave wool tapestries done by Mark Adams. This time I had only ten minutes to get to my next plane, but it seemed worth the effort to hurry over to the tapestries for just a moment's look at their beauty. To my great delight, I then learned that my plane would be leaving a few minutes late, so I returned to the wall hangings, sat on the floor in front of them, and enjoyed for seven full minutes their exquisite, many-colored varieties of flowers. A gentleman passed by and asked, "Are you all right?" I laughed and told him that I particularly loved looking at the beautiful flowers, but afterward it made me sad to think about how rarely people dwell on beauty in our society. Furthermore, the Sabbath *shalom* created by those few minutes of intense delight in the beauty of the tapestries carried me through the rest of the evening despite the subsequent hassles, the ferocious ear pain I experienced on the plane trip, and an unusually long wait for a ride home from the airport.

Besides these kinds of beauty—of the temple where we worship corporately, of our homes, of literature and art—the beauty of the larger temple of nature offers another way to enjoy Sabbath keeping. We must be very careful with this idea, however, for there is a dangerous temptation to worship the creation itself instead of its Creator. As long as we keep our perspective, Sabbath time spent enjoying the beauty of nature can be a very worshipful experience.

When I was a child, one of my family's favorite Sunday-afternoon activities in the fall was taking a hike along the Maumee River (in northwest Ohio) to enjoy the colors of the leaves. I was sure that every year was more beautiful than the last. The activity was especially wonderful because it took my parents away from the work that consumed most of their time, and it gave my two older brothers and me a memorably enjoyable afternoon together with them. During my years in graduate school in Indiana, many happy memories came back to me on Sunday afternoons when I rode my ramshackle bike or walked through the fall splendor in the parks. When we build family memories of delightful Sabbath times together, those become part of the heritage of our children and not only give them ideas for their own adult Sabbath observances, but also flood those observances with happy memories.

Besides all this, enjoying the beauties of nature outside stirs our sense of our own beauty. For some reason, every time I come into the house with pink cheeks from walking in the brisk autumn air or with tingly muscles from playing in the snow, I feel better about myself physically. Moreover, not only the physical relaxation but also the emotional and spiritual healing that take place in our enjoyment of nature give us a greater awareness of the beauty within ourselves.

In a larger sense, the whole practice of Sabbath keeping makes me feel more beautiful. As I spend the day reflecting on the character of God, I am overwhelmed by his love for me. As I feast upon his goodness in all its beautiful forms, I realize more profoundly that I am a special part of his creation and designed especially for his purposes in a uniquely beautiful way.

So it is with many of the other dimensions of Sabbath keeping outlined in this book. When we rest in our own personalities, it helps us gain a better sense of our social sexuality. When we try to make things lovely in order to keep the Sabbath, it deepens our own loveliness. When we try to gift others with delightful Sabbath experiences, that effort deepens the splendor of our relationships. When we spend some of our Sabbath time enjoying art or music or literature, we appreciate more fully our own sensitivities and creative gifts.

Concentrating on beauty, especially in terms of light, has long been a part of the Jewish Sabbath liturgy. The traditional home service for Sabbath eve begins with this prayer:

> Blessed art Thou, O Lord our God, King of the universe, who hast sanctified us by Thy commandments, and commanded us to kindle the Sabbath lights.
>
> May the Sabbath-light which illumines our dwelling cause peace and happiness to shine in our home. Bless us,

O God, on this holy Sabbath, and cause Thy divine glory to shine upon us. Enlighten our darkness and guide us and all mankind, Thy children, towards truth and eternal light. Amen.

Similarly, a "Reform Home Service for Sabbath Eve" includes the following paragraph in its Kiddush ritual:

Come, let us welcome the Sabbath in joy and peace! Like a bride, radiant and joyous, comes the Sabbath. It brings blessings to our hearts; workday thoughts and cares are put aside. The brightness of the Sabbath light shines forth to tell that the divine spirit of love abides within our home. In that light all our blessings are enriched, all our griefs and trials are softened.[3]

So, too, may our Christian observances of the Sabbath be filled with light and loveliness, so that the radiance and Joy of the day can soften our griefs and trials and bring beauty to the other days of our weeks.

3. Abraham E. Millgram, *Sabbath: The Day of Delight* (Philadelphia: Jewish Publication Society of America, 5725/1965), pp. 24, 67.

25. Feasting with Food

JUST RECENTLY WE CELEBRATED THANKSGIVING DAY here in the United States, and the holiday resting gave me a chance to reflect on the concept of feasting as it is most commonly understood in our society. I think it is very sad that for many people to feast means to make gluttons out of themselves.

Because of that introductory remark, you might expect that I will argue for a Sabbath of fasting and pious religious asceticism. Actually—delightfully—the opposite is the case. In contrast to what we might expect, the Sabbath is a day for feasting, but feasting in the best sense of the word. In general, Americans don't know how to feast because they don't know how to fast.

Sabbath feasting—celebration—draws its meaning because of its contrast to the fasting—the simple life—of the other six days. Even in their poorest times, the Jews make every effort to buy the special foods and candles that mark the keeping of the Sabbath. Throughout their history, many have been willing to go without things during the week in order to purchase the customary items for the Sabbath feast. They honor the day by enjoying special meals prepared ahead of time so that their delight is not marred by any work. Furthermore, as the anthropological study *Life Is with*

People emphasizes, "the delicacies of the Sabbath are enjoyed slowly, with time to appreciate each mouthful, and with pauses between each course" for learned conversation and for asking questions of the family's guests. The mother is rewarded with special compliments for her skill in preparing the meal.[1]

If we lived more simply most of the time, our feasts would be distinctive events. As it is, since most Americans have all kinds of special things to eat every day, for many the only way to make Thanksgiving and Christmas feasts uncommon is by eating more. It would be good if we could restore the concept of feasting not as something to regret (don't we all have to lose a few pounds after the Thanksgiving, Christmas, and New Year's season?), but as a delight.[2]

At one especially fulfilling point in my life, my job was an experiment in campus ministry funded by a few members of a small Lutheran congregation serving two university towns. My grocery budget had to be minimal for several months—until this mission congregation was given extra subsidy funds to finance my position. I learned a lot about feasting because of two extraordinary events that occurred during those months.

The first involved a former student who came over one evening and said he had a problem. I told him I would be glad to help him if I could, and he replied, "Oh, you definitely can!" His wonderful problem was that he had shot a deer (legally) while bow hunting and didn't know what to do with the meat. A friend in the congregation I was serving lent me space in a freezer locker to store the deer meat so that I could use it whenever I wanted to host a real celebration for guests. Because most of the rest of my meals had to be simple, those parties with deer meat were

---

1. Mark Zborowski and Elizabeth Herzog, *Life Is with People: The Culture of the Shtetl* (New York: Schocken Books, 1952), p. 47.

2. A delightful advocate of holy celebration in the kitchen is Jeff Smith, a former university chaplain who owned a restaurant called The Chaplain's Pantry in Tacoma and who has published *The Frugal Gourmet* (New York: William Morrow, 1984) and *The Frugal Gourmet Cooks with Wine* (New York: William Morrow, 1986).

spectacular occasions. Sometimes I regret that I have more money now, because in those frugal days all those special occasions were like major holidays. (I really should write "holy days.")

The other event stands out in my mind because once, before the advent of the deer, I opened my grocery envelope to get some funds for shopping and found it empty. The end of the month was near, but not near enough for me to receive my next paycheck to buy the groceries I needed. I went to work that day not a little frustrated. Midmorning I found in the church mailbox an envelope addressed to me, but with no return address. Inside was a ten-dollar bill—a simple gift that made an enormous difference in my whole attitude. In a mysteriously miraculous way God had provided for me.

How did the person who sent that money know that I especially needed it at that point in time? That event indelibly imprinted on my mind and spirit the realization that God provides for us in amazing ways. It also made me more keenly aware of the hundreds of millions of people for whom God's provision is blocked by human greed, political machinations, and the other injustices of this world. Our experiences of God's grace and care challenge us all the more deeply to become actively involved in local, national, and international agencies working to feed the hungry and to rectify the tragic injustices of global economics.

Many of those who suffer in poverty, however, know better than we rich Americans the delight of God's provision. I recently read the true story of a young American woman who spent time in Nicaragua with a peasant woman. Many years of war had destroyed numerous crops, and now insects were threatening the corn. The two women harvested all they could, but the American was shocked and angry when the peasant woman kept giving away corn to everyone they met as they walked home. By the time they arrived, only four ears remained for their only meal of the day. To the American's great surprise, however, throughout the rest of the season she and her hostess had enough to eat—because of the similar generosity of many neighbors and friends.

This point is worth repeating: when we are not forced to live simply, we lose track of the wonder of God's provision. That is one of the reasons the Jews make a determined effort to serve distinctive foods for their Sabbath celebrations. It reminds them of how God provided for their Sabbaths in the wilderness by increasing the amount of manna on Friday mornings and by keeping it from spoiling on Friday nights, though every other night of the week it would get wormy if they tried to hoard it.

One way to increase our sense of the delight of the Sabbath day is by eating more simply during the week and saving favorite foods for our holy celebrations. It might seem silly, but eating oatmeal for breakfast every weekday and then enjoying English muffins or an omelette on the Sabbath has really been an important part of my Sabbath keeping during the past few years. That way, the very simple ritual of eating breakfast reminds me that this is a special day to be intentionally appreciated.

To choose to reserve for Sabbath times some things that are exceptional in our families merely requires a little planning. To have cocoa for breakfast instead of tea, to eat out with friends or host a dinner party or plan a potluck for a congregational care group, to enjoy one's favorite foods only on Sunday, even to use especially precious bowls or mugs—these are a few simple examples of intentional ways to mark the Sabbath as a time for feasting, as a day of delight.

Of course, Christians specifically enjoy the feast of the Holy Eucharist as part of their Sabbath commemoration. Having become accustomed to celebrating the Lord's Supper every Sunday, I was disappointed in the last few years to find that communion was not a central part of weekly worship in the congregation in which I was participating. The early Christians described in Acts 2:42-47 loved to be together and often broke bread together in their homes to remember the death and resurrection of Christ. Those of us who do not celebrate this feast often in our congregations might question the reason for this lack of frequency. Those of us who do celebrate it often might question whether it has become an empty routine or if it does truly communicate to us the eschatological delight of Sabbath feasting. Since in the Lord's Supper we look forward to Christ's coming again and to the eternal feasting we will enjoy in his presence, the frequent celebration of the Eucharist (when it is not an empty routine) gives us a foretaste of that Joy.

One of the most important reasons for restoring a proper sense of feasting is so that we can be more responsible about caring for the hungry. If we are gluttons all of the time, we do not know what it means to go without luxury, much less the essentials. If we consciously choose to live more simply most of the time so that our Sabbath feasting is a holy celebration, then we are aware of how special those holy occasions are. Inevitably this will lead to a greater concern for those who are never able to feast, for those whose very lives are threatened by our gluttony.

One might wonder how I can talk about feasting as part of our Sabbath keeping and about concern for the hungry in the same chapter. The two seem to be mutually exclusive. How can we possibly enjoy our feasting if we are aware that others are starving—that, indeed, forty thousand people die of malnutrition and related diseases every day?

One of my friends who is a doctor helped me understand the correlation between the two because of the experiences she had while serving in India. Whenever a child was born, the family would spend a great proportion of their money to buy the celebrative foods used in India to mark such momentous occasions. At times Janet would protest and want to pay for things so that the family would not have to use their scant resources. But they would always protest: How did she dare spoil their privilege of spending their money to create a celebration for this special occasion? What is money for, but to use well?

Because I grew up with little money, I tend to be a very good steward of my financial resources. However, the result is that I fall into the opposite sin as far as the power of Mammon is concerned. I become such a good steward that I lose sight of grace. I am hesitant to give my money freely to someone who might need it, but might not spend it as wisely as I would. In his forthright book entitled *Money and Power,* Jacques Ellul exposes the sin of this fault, which is the direct opposite of profligacy. We let money become a god in our lives just as much by being overly anxious and tightfisted about spending it as by wanting lots of it or by worrying about getting enough of it.[3]

As Ellul recommends, the best way to combat the power of Mammon is to profane money, to take away its sacred character by spending it wisely, but also by giving it freely and graciously. This ties in with the command given to the Hebrew people about the use of their tithes. Deuteronomy 14:22-29 lists three main ways in which the tithes of the Israelites' fields should be used. The tithes were first of all to be used for their own celebration. The second and third beneficiaries of the offerings were "the Levites," who had no land allotment of their own, but served instead by leading the worship of the people (in other words, the professional church workers), and "the aliens, the fatherless and the widows" who had no other way to find provision (in other words, the recipients of welfare, in the best sense of that term). These are the instructions:

> Be sure to set aside a tenth of all that your fields produce each year. Eat the tithe of your grain, new wine and oil, and the firstborn of your herds and flocks in the presence of the LORD your God at the place he will choose as a dwelling for his Name, so that you may learn to revere the LORD your God always. But if that place is too distant and you have been blessed by the LORD your God and cannot carry your tithe (because the place where the LORD will choose to put his Name is so far away), then exchange your tithe for silver, and take the silver with you and go to the place the LORD your God will choose. Use the silver to buy whatever you like: cattle, sheep, wine or other fermented drink, or anything you wish. Then you and your household shall eat there in the presence of the LORD your God and rejoice. And do not neglect the Levites living in your towns, for they have no allotment or inheritance of their own.

---

3. See Ellul, *Money and Power,* trans. LaVonne Neff (Downers Grove, Ill.: InterVarsity Press, 1984), especially pp. 106-16.

> At the end of every three years, bring all the tithes of that year's produce and store it in your towns, so that the Levites (who have no allotment or inheritance of their own) and the aliens, the fatherless and the widows who live in your towns may come and eat and be satisfied, and so that the LORD your God may bless you in all the work of your hands.

I don't know of many Christian communities that actually tithe, much less spend that money as God instructs. Notice that none of the tithes was used for the place of worship! When God gave the wandering children of Israel plans to construct the tabernacle, the people responded with such Joy to the invitation to bring special gifts for its construction that Moses had to tell them to stop bringing things (Exod. 36:5-7).

Rather than using the tithes of the community for the sanctuary (which is built instead by the special extra offerings of the people—perhaps offerings of their building skills or artistic works), we are instructed to use the tithes for celebrations, for professional church workers (how richly our congregational programs could be expanded if we had plenty of staff to "equip the saints for ministry"!), and for the poor. If we used our funds in such a way, we would have more than enough to care for the poor as well as to honor God by our worship celebrations.

If we celebrate the Sabbath with special foods, we will be more conscious of the poor, and, if we spend our lives caring for the poor, our Sabbath festivities will be more meaningful. Americans do not know how to feast because they do not know how to fast. Especially if we fast on behalf of those who don't have enough and share our plenty with them, our feasting will be much more meaningful.

The same is doubly true when we share our Sabbath feasting with friends or strangers. To invite others to keep the Sabbath together with us gives us the opportunity to teach them also about feasting and fasting. To invite those who cannot return the invitation (as we are challenged to do in Luke 14:13-14) enables us to share our Sabbath celebration with those who might not otherwise have any way to feast. That is why I appreciate so much the efforts of Broadway Christian Parish in South Bend (see Chapter 16) as they continue to invite the neighborhood for Sunday noon dinner. What a wonderful way to teach our children the meaning of Sabbath keeping and to help them learn the delight of a Sabbath-week rhythm of fasting and feasting.

The Jewish understanding of the Sabbath brings together the rhythm of fasting and feasting with a concern for the poor and a recognition of God's gracious provision. *Life Is with People* offers this description:

> Sabbath brings the joy of the future life into the shtetl. This is the climax of the week, "a different world, no worry, no work." . . . Any delicacy that one finds during the week should be bought and kept, if possible, "for Sabbath."
>
> . . . None must work, none must mourn, none must worry, none must hunger on that day. Any Jew who lacks a Sabbath meal should be helped by those who have more than he. But of course one hopes not to need help, for no matter how poor a man may be he counts on the Lord to provide for the Sabbath meal. Some stroke of luck, some sudden opportunity to earn the price of a fish. . . . Many stories and legends describe miracles by which God at the last moment provided Sabbath fare for a devout Jew who lacked means to "make Sabbath."
>
> . . . Whoever he is, any stranger in need will come to the synagogue on Friday evening and at the end of the service he will expect to be invited to some home. . . . There is a legend that every Sabbath God sends the prophet Elijah, dressed as a needy stranger, to visit the Jews and observe the way they are fulfilling His Commandments. Accordingly the stranger one brings home may be the prophet. No legend is required, however, to stimulate Sabbath hospitality. Prophet or beggar, to feed the hungry is a "good deed." . . . Therefore, it is a privilege to share the Sabbath feast, even if by ill luck it is a meager one.[4]

---

4. Zborowski and Herzog, *Life Is with People,* pp. 37-38, 44-45.

FEASTING

We fast so that we can more profoundly enjoy the feast. We do all that we can to make the feast special. We share our feast with those in need. And we look for God's surprises in the way he provides for us and in the poor guest who brings us his presence.

26. Feasting with Affection

ONE OF THE MOST TERRIFYING ASPECTS of the technological society is its loss of intimacy. Many people in our culture are desperate for affection, and most do not know how to give or receive it. To keep the Sabbath offers us the possibility for learning to deepen our relationships and to embrace others with godly affection.

Sabbath keeping offers us hope for relationships because of its emphasis on one's relationship with God, its rhythms of community and solitude, its gift of time, and its call to cease striving and productivity and work. Furthermore, the intentionality of the day lends itself to a conscious enjoyment of our relationships with, and delight in, each other as the outgrowth of our delight in Yahweh.

Earlier we discussed the fact that the image of God involves relationship (see Chapter 6). God said, "Let *us* make [humankind] in *our* image," and in the image of God he created *them,* male and female (Gen. 1:26-27, my emphasis). Moreover, the beginning Genesis narratives emphasize that God wanted a personal relationship with the people he had created. He walked in their garden and sought them (Gen. 3:8-9).

189

The theme of God's presence fills all of the Scriptures—those of the Hebrew people as well as those of the early Christian Church. All the narratives about the beginnings of Israel include promises from Yahweh to be with his people—from Yahweh's first promise to Abram in Genesis 12:1 to *show* him the land; through Yahweh's promise to Moses in Exodus 6:6-8 that he would take the Israelites as his own people, to be their God and to bring them into the land; to Yahweh's promise in Joshua 1:5 and 9 that he would be with Joshua as he had been with Moses.

In the New Testament the theme continues to be prominent—appearing in such places as Jesus' final words to the disciples that he would be with them always to the close of the age (Matt. 28:20) and in the repeated assurances to the apostle Paul recorded in the Book of Acts (see, for example, Acts 23:11 and 27:23-25). In addition, Paul frequently begins or ends his letters with the comfort that God and his grace will be with the people whom he addresses (see, for example, Philippians 4:9b and Romans 16:20b).

As we have stressed throughout this book, one of the principal goals of Sabbath keeping is to set aside time for feasting on this presence of God. By spending a day enjoying the company of Yahweh, we learn more and more to delight in his character and the gifts of his grace. Furthermore, the growth of that relationship inevitably leads to a deepening of our relationships with others of his people. This frequently used image is wonderfully true: our relationships are like the spokes of a wheel—the closer we draw to the center, which is God, the closer we are to the other spokes.

Our feasting on the presence of God involves the rhythm of solitude and community within the framework of our Sabbath keeping. We need some time alone for contemplation and prayer, but we also participate in the corporate worship of the day, which is a major component in the deepening of our relationships within the congregational community.

Worship offers a multiplicity of opportunities for feasting in relationships. We repent together for our failures and receive the forgiveness for which the corporate body of the Church is responsible (John 20:21-23). We sing together and join our hearts and voices in praise. We pray about the concerns of others and commit ourselves to continued support of them during the week to come. We hear the results of our prayers, celebrate together the answers that God has given, and weep together over the sadnesses of this strange world. We pass to each other the handshake or embrace or kiss of peace. We feast together in the Holy Supper that calls us to discern therein the true body of Christ, which nourishes his Body, the Church.

One of the greatest gifts of Sabbath keeping is its gift of time. I cherished those Sunday-afternoon hikes along the river with my family because they gave me moments of closeness with my father, who was usually gone in the evenings during the week for the work of the congregation that he served as school principal. Sunday evening "hot dogs by the fireplace" afforded the same privilege.

When we set aside a whole day to cease the work of the week, we accept the gift of time for visits and hospitality. I loved the freedom of Sundays especially during graduate school because, if I was invited to dinner at someone's home, I never had to worry about getting back to read a book or write a paper, since I simply did not do those things on the Sabbath day. Instead, I could relax and enjoy the company of my hosts, receive their affection, and express my affection more tenderly to them.

That same freedom pervades my own home when the Sabbath gives me adequate time for hospitality. There is no need for any rush, no pressure to get rid of guests after awhile in order to get some work done. Instead, the gift of time to explore at a leisurely pace promotes carefulness, discovery, and plumbing the depths of relationships. Sabbath time frees us from any need for haste. Chaim Grade, author of *My Mother's Sabbath Days*, writes of a Hebrew wall clock, the pendulum of which "swings back and forth sedately, as though it too wishes to avoid haste on the Sabbath"![1] Such a freedom from frenzy invites knowing without panic, true intimacy without the pressure of other expectations.

We who are God's people can teach the rest of the world that intimacy involves every aspect of our beings. Not only did God design physical intimacy, culminating in the sacred union of a man and a woman in marriage, but also he has created us with minds, spirits, and souls that we can share deeply with others. Sabbath time enables us to experience deeper affection by giving us opportunities to share closely with our loved ones our thoughts, prayers, desires, emotions, disappointments, intentions, and values.

Furthermore, the call of the Sabbath day to cease our work and striving and productivity gives us time for such inefficient things as sitting quietly together and enjoying one another's company, writing letters or making phone calls to distant loved ones, and thinking about others and spending extra time in prayer for them or making gifts for them. Jews include in their customs big celebratory meals in which they sit around the table singing, arguing points of Torah, and sharing wine and good food—all of which draw people more intimately together. In addition, rabbinic guidelines include an injunction that married people should have sex on the Sabbath.[2] Since I am single, I do not enjoy that special privilege, but the freedom of Sabbath time always makes me feel more able to express my love, and it opens up my own creativity to discover new ways to be more affectionate with my friends and family.

The Scriptures invite godly affection within the Christian community. The intimacy enjoined in Paul's exhortation to the Romans to "love each other with brotherly [and sisterly] affection" is kept pure by his next phrase, "and take delight in honor-

---

1. Grade, *My Mother's Sabbath Days: A Memoir*, trans. Channa Kleinerman Goldstein and Inna Hecker Grade (New York: Alfred A. Knopf, 1986), p. 11.
2. "Try Shabbas" (editorial), *Tikkun* 3 (Jan./Feb. 1988): 13.

ing each other" (Rom. 12:10, J. B. Phillips' *New Testament in Modern English*). Indeed, the Christian community has much to offer the world as an alternative society full of honorable affection and intimacy. So many people in our society are so starved for affection that they seek it in false—and immoral—ways. When members of the Christian community treat one another with holy affection, they meet the need for intimacy and enfold each other in the embrace of God.

I remember one Sunday afternoon in particular many years ago when I was feeling very lonely and alienated. After worship and away from the setting of our parish building, I ran into one of the members of my congregation. He came over and gave me a great big hug and a kiss on the cheek and said, "I've missed you." His affection kept me warm all day, and even now as I remember the occasion I continue to feel loved and accepted.

Moreover, the intentionality of the Sabbath day lends itself to a conscious enjoyment of our relationships and delight in one another as the outgrowth of our delight in Yahweh. I am amazed at how much harder it is to get angry with others in the graciousness of time on the Sabbath. On the other hand, it is incredibly wonderful to have the opportunity to get to know one another on deeper levels than are possible in the weekday rush of life.

Affection takes time. In the mad rush of our society's pace, everything gets turned backwards. People jump into bed together to get to know one another instead of choosing committed sexual communion as the culmination of a long process of establishing intimacy on many other levels. The Christian community as an alternative society can promote social intimacy in various dimensions of life by offering opportunities for Sabbath fellowship in worship, meals, activities, programs, and possibilities for service. We as individuals can choose to spend our time building careful intimacy with friends and relatives through sharing our deepest thoughts and feelings, giving gifts, and doing favors for each other, as well as through gentle touches, enfolding hugs, and tender kisses.

Sabbath keeping offers a holy time for needed silence and

contemplation, as well as a time for joint celebration. In its rhythm of solitude and community it brings us healing for our deepest needs by teaching us the love of God and then giving us a community to love and by which we are loved. Out of the silence of our communion with God and within the support of our caring Christian community, we are enabled to reach out affectionately to those around us who need our caring tenderness.

27. Feasting and Festival

IN AUGUST OF 1964, Jean Vanier, a French philosopher, began the experiment of living in a covenant community together with some handicapped men. Since then, his continued creation of l'Arche (the Ark) homes for the mentally and emotionally handicapped in Europe, North America, and the Third World has captured the interest of many, for, in his experiences of sharing intimately with those considered incapable of normal human life, Vanier has discovered that the "deficient" ones serve profoundly as his teachers. One of the most important things that they know how to do is celebrate. Residents of l'Arche communities commemorate each other's birthdays, other important events in their lives, and special blessings that come to the home. And if there isn't a reason for merriment on a particular day, they make one up!

In his book about l'Arche, Michael Downey emphasizes that the celebrations there continue "no matter how deep the suffering"—that, in fact, the celebration "intensifies as the suffering is recognized and appropriated." Moreover, celebration at l'Arche "flows very easily into prayer."[1] The handicapped teach

---

1. Downey, *A Blessed Weakness: The Spirit of Jean Vanier and l'Arche* (San Francisco: Harper & Row, 1986), p. 85.

us this important lesson: We do not need to wait until suffering is over to celebrate, and the festivity itself deepens our communication with God. For this reason, to keep the Sabbath necessarily has involved celebration—even in times when the Jews were being persecuted. To continue to observe the festival of the Sabbath enabled many of them to maintain great courage in the death camps of the Holocaust.

As Downey stresses, celebration is not a *compensation* for suffering. Rather, "Joy born of deep suffering is nourished by moments of celebration. . . . Celebration properly understood is the acceptance of life in an ever growing recognition that it is so precious."[2]

Our society has forgotten how to celebrate. It has associated celebration with dissipation. It has turned the festival of the birth of Christ into a gluttonous spending spree and the festival of the resurrection of Christ into a spring egg-roll and candy-hunt. These occasions now nurture in children not a sense of the holy God, but a selfish desire to possess. Such acquisitiveness can never lead to true celebration, for the latter is inherently turned outward.

We cannot celebrate ourselves; we can only celebrate others. As friends and relatives mark the passing of another year, we celebrate the gift of their birth. As we prepare for the holy days, we ready our hearts and spirits for the thanksgiving and praise of the occasion—so that we can celebrate God's gifts of himself and his grace. In the context of asking how we can pass our faith along to the next generation, Sara Wenger Shenk, author of *Why Not Celebrate!* defines celebration as follows:

> How do we celebrate peoplehood? How do we celebrate God's good earth? How do our children develop a sense of identity that runs deeper than the latest fad? How can we give them a heritage with firmer roots than the current peer group?
>
> These are questions that go to the heart of what

---

2. Downey, *A Blessed Weakness,* p. 83.

celebration is about. Celebration is the honoring of that which we hold most dear. Celebration is delighting in that which tells us who we are. Celebration is taking the time to cherish each other. Celebration is returning with open arms and thankful hearts to our Maker.[3]

Sabbath keeping offers us a unique opportunity to celebrate, for what we commemorate is God's constancy and consistency, his order and faithfulness, the preciousness of life under his sovereignty. It is not like our birthdays, which we celebrate because they happen only once a year. Rather, we celebrate every seven days because God's grace happens always.

I once thought that if I made every Sabbath day a festival, week after week of such celebrations would cause them to become routine and meaningless. However, to my great delight, that has not proved to be the case. Instead, each celebration has its own special characteristics, but the thread of the festival's weekly occurrence provides some unity and continuity. The result is that the Sabbath celebration carries over into the attitudes and spirit of the workweek. Truly, as we have previously noted, the whole week derives its character from the Sabbath day. The effects of Sabbath keeping are manifest in all kinds of transformations.

For example, the deepened affection of Sabbath keeping continues throughout the week, even in the rush of busy-ness which allows no time for particular expressions of affection. (By this comment I do not at all mean to give excuse to those who never take the time to be affectionate during the week. What I mean is that the consciousness of Sabbath affection gives our care for one another some staying power that's helpful in times of extreme pressure or even of crisis.) Furthermore, our own sense of being loved by God motivates us to continue loving even when we do not receive affection in response.

There are many ways, in which the Sabbath provides op-

---

3. Shenk, *Why Not Celebrate!* (Intercourse, Penn.: Good Books, 1987), pp. 2-3.

portunities for festival celebration. Most important of all is the worship time. We celebrate each other as we gather together for corporate worship, but especially we celebrate the gifts of God in our thanksgiving and praise. In the Lord's Supper we celebrate his passion and death until he comes; then we will celebrate perfectly and forever the Joy of his presence. The Scripture lessons that are read celebrate the events in our history as God's people. We listen to the accounts of Yahweh's intervention in the lives of the children of Israel and of the early Christians, and these narrative reminders prompt us to remember our own history of redemption. We pay attention to Yahweh's instructions to us for living according to his wisdom, and we receive guidance for our daily lives. The promises proclaimed stir up in us eager anticipation of their fulfillment in the future and gratitude for God's faithfulness on our behalf. To hear the stories of God's care for his people gives us myriads of reasons to celebrate, so every worship service becomes a special festival of some specific aspect of God's provision.

Certain traditions of preparation make each Sabbath a festival. Sunday was always special in my childhood simply because of the delight of anticipation in our family's customary Saturday-night tasks—for me, those included taking a special bath, curling my hair, and setting out my best clothes to wear in the morning. I wish every child could grow up with that sense of delight in expectation of holy worship. The very habits of my home imbued me with a sense of the holy.

Festival involves the paradoxical combination of tradition and creativity. Our Sabbath customs—making certain preparations of the home and of food the day before, lighting Kiddush candles at the beginning, worshiping, enjoying special meals, lighting Havdalah candles and saying prayers at the end—become the framework of tradition into which we can pour all our creativity. Each Sabbath becomes its own unique celebration as we compose new songs, play new instruments, plan new menus for the feasts, articulate new prayers, design new activities, discover new forms to express our affection, think new ideas about

God—and do all these things to honor him and to experience his presence in a special way.

Festival also means the heightened involvement of our senses. As part of our Sabbath keeping we open our eyes in new ways to gaze in wonder at the beauty of God's creation—in nature, in works of art, in people. We open our ears afresh to hear the thrilling good news of God's love and grace as it comes to us in Word and worship, in concerts and the songs of birds, in rollicking laughter and chuckles of delight, in the breathing of those we love as we sit close beside them. We taste God's goodness in the bread and wine of communion, in the unusual flavors of special Sabbath foods, in the crisp air on our walk. We smell the sweet perfume of Sabbath peace in the fragrances of worship incense, of flowers, of burning logs or glowing candles, of meals baking in the oven. We touch the tenderness of God in the hugs and kisses of our loved ones, in the familiar binding of the Bible that we read, in the physical sensation of well-being as we walk and talk with friends or plunge into the stimulating waters of a lake, in the sweet breeze as we picnic on its shores, in the intimacy of such shared special moments and activities.

Festival also includes the paradoxical combination of memory and anticipation. We see this especially in the festival of the Lord's Supper, in which we "remember the Lord's death until he comes" (a wonderful combination of the past and the future in our present experience!). The Sabbath is an intentional day of remembering how Yahweh ordained the practice of Sabbath keeping by his own example at Creation, how the people of Israel observed it throughout their history, and how Jesus continued to practice it and to honor it, especially in his acts of compassion. Moreover, to keep the Sabbath is also to look to the future, when we will finally know the perfect ceasing of all work, the ultimate resting in the completion of God's purposes, the total embracing of all God's best gifts, and the eternal feasting in the very presence of our Lord.

Sabbath keeping also involves looking ahead to the next

festival and thereby causing everything that occurs in the week between to be oriented around our relationship with God. The movement from one climax of the Sabbath to the next enables us to set our minds on things above (as we are urged to do in Colossians 3:1-4) without becoming so heavenly minded that we are no earthly good. A Sabbath focus, as we have previously emphasized, does not remove us from the world; it simply gives us a larger perspective for plunging into its needs and sufferings more deeply.

For example, our Sabbath feasting challenges us to become more involved in providing food for the hungry and economic possibilities for the oppressed. Our experience of the peace of God's presence in our Sabbath worship and our listening to Scripture texts that proclaim God's purposes of peace motivate us to become more active in working for peace in the world— serving as agents of reconciliation in our offices and neighborhoods, voting for local and national political candidates who will work for global peace, contributing to agencies that build peace by establishing justice. Our celebration of the Sabbath festival gives us hope and strength and power for dealing with all the work and events of the week to come in worshipful ways. Most of all, Sabbath celebration gives us a deep sense of the Joy that is ours because of the resurrection of Christ, and that festival Joy equips us to glorify God in whatever tasks we might undertake in the following six days.

That is one of the reasons that I prefer to keep the Sabbath on Sunday—because it combines the festival of the Resurrection with the tradition of a whole day set apart to imitate the Creator in his resting. It brings together both sides of my heritage—my roots in Judaica, in the faith of my forebears among the people of Israel, and my roots in the traditions of the believers in Christ who followed him when he walked on this earth. I don't want to lose either side of that heritage: that is why it is especially important to me not to lose the practice of keeping the Sabbath, even though I celebrate the Lord's Day on the day associated with his resurrection.

Hanging in my study is a picture of the laughing Christ. I love this picture because it shows a side of Jesus that I don't usually think about. During my years in graduate school, seeing this picture over my desk put everything into perspective wonderfully. All our human pretensions at brilliance are probably quite laughable in Christ's eyes.

This painting especially captures for me the essence of Sabbath keeping. God certainly never intended the day to be one of boring rituals, empty rites, oppressive restrictions, or condemning legalism. Jesus probably had a good time healing people, and perhaps his very delight in doing so aroused the ire of his critics. His humor usually escapes us, but many of the stories he told to describe the kingdom of God are absolutely hilarious; imagine a smoking bedmat about to burst into flames because someone tried to hide a light under it! (Luke 8:16). Jesus no doubt enjoyed the children immensely when he touched them and blessed them and enfolded them in his arms (Mark 10:13-16). I wonder if he tickled them. As Jesus has shown us by his example, our relationship with God and, thus, with his people can be a great source of delight. Our Sabbath keeping is to be a great adventure of fun.

I remember especially one Sunday when I was visiting my goddaughter and her family in California. Another friend drove over, and we spent the afternoon in the pool. During the week I swim vigorous laps to take care of my health. However, Sabbath keeping includes ceasing to work, so on this particular day I just enjoyed playing with the children in the water. After they got out, my friend and I continued for a long time to play "knock the other one off the rubber raft" and other silly games. The whole afternoon was sheer delight and full of more laughter than I had experienced in months.

Children are especially good at keeping us young and teaching us how to play. Consequently, we need their partnership to learn the full meaning of Sabbath festivity. In "Partnership with Children," Hal Miller even suggests that, as a temporary alternative to Sunday school, we should let our children play with adult friends.[4] That would certainly be more of a Sabbath rest for them and would contribute to the entire Christian community's ability to take delight in the Sabbath celebration.

Jesus said that only those who are as children can enter the kingdom of God. Although there are many theological interpretations of his comment—ranging from the idea that children were the least important human beings in that society (indicating the need for humility) to the notions of childlike trust or neediness (indicating the glad acceptance of grace)—perhaps we could also translate it as "only those who play . . ."! I think of the musical score of Aaron Copland's ballet *Appalachian Spring*, with its folk song, "'Tis a Gift to Be Simple; 'Tis a Gift to Be Free," and its story of how the hardship and poverty of a newly married couple are mitigated by the simple pleasures of dancing and play.

Most of the days of the week we do what we have to do, what is expected of us. Sabbath keeping frees us to take delight in everything, to uncork our own spontaneity. Because there is nothing we *have* to do, we are free suddenly to say yes to invitations, to read fairy tales, to be children, to discover the presence of God hidden all around us. To keep the Sabbath invites us to have festival fun, to play, to enjoy our guests and our activities, to relish the opportunity for worship, to celebrate the eternal presence of God himself. We feast in every aspect of our being— physical, intellectual, social, emotional, spiritual—and we feast with music, beauty, food, and affection. Our bodies, minds, souls, and spirits celebrate together with others that God is in our midst.

---

4. Miller, "Partnership with Children," *Voices in the Wilderness* 2 (July/Aug. 1987): 7.

28. *Sabbath Ceasing, Resting, Embracing, and Feasting*

To KEEP THE SABBATH means to cherish it, to honor it as the Queen of our days, in consort with the King of the Universe. To develop the habit of Sabbath keeping requires some intentionality on our part, but ultimately it sets us free from any sort of legalism. Its ordering sets us free to be creative. Its ceasing enables us to rest; its feasting enables us to embrace afresh.

All the great motifs of our Christian faith are underscored in our Sabbath keeping. Its Ceasing deepens our repentance for the many ways that we fail to trust God and try to create our own future. Its Resting strengthens our faith in the totality of his grace. Its Embracing invites us to take the truths of our faith and apply them practically in our values and lifestyles. Its Feasting heightens our sense of eschatological hope—the Joy of our present experience of God's love and its foretaste of the Joy to come.

Even Jews are recognizing that Sabbath keeping is a wonderful tradition that needs to be discovered anew. An editorial in the journal *Tikkun,* a bimonthly "Jewish Critique of Politics, Culture and Society," asserts,

You don't have to be Jewish to learn from Judaism's most spectacularly wise observance: the sabbath, Shabbat, the day of rest.

Yet most Jews have no idea of the psychological and spiritual sophistication built into this observance—mostly because they've never tried it. [Then the editorial describes false images of the Sabbath.] . . .

Yet if Jews were to discover Shabbat in someone else's spiritual or religious practices, the chances are we would find it deeply intriguing and persuasive.

The idea underlying much of the ritual observance is this: For six days a week human beings are involved in the act of making, shaping, and transforming the world. So, we take one solid period of time, twenty-four hours, to change our relationship to the world—to refrain from acting upon it [Ceasing] and, instead, to stand back and celebrate the grandeur and mystery of creation.

Shabbat ritual is designed to disconnect us from our normal attitude of making, doing, changing material existence, and to connect us to the realm of time [Resting]. To experience the world free from the need to interfere with it is a transformative and liberating experience. But it can't be achieved in the midst of a day filled with getting, spending, and making. This is where the rituals come in. Like the guides to any deep meditation process, the rituals are the accumulated wisdom of many generations on how to most effectively "get into" the experience.

. . . It is the immersion in this experience [the "old formula" of "a complete twenty-four-hour period of separation from the demands of the world"] that provides the refreshment of soul that is so sadly absent from most political communities [Embracing]. But unlike various spiritual paths that have been imported from the East, Shabbat is celebrated in community [Feasting] and not by isolated individuals, and its focus is political, leading one out of the Sabbath and back into the struggle to remake the world.[1]

---

1. "Try Shabbas" (editorial), *Tikkun* 3 (Jan./Feb. 1988): 12-13.

A few practical suggestions might be helpful as we bring this discussion to a close and address the need to apply a theology of ceasing, resting, embracing, and feasting to our own spiritual disciplines and weekly lives.

First of all, it is foundational to *decide* that you want to keep the Sabbath. You can add, modify, even delete certain practices as your customs develop, but the important beginning point is to be adamant about the day—that it *will* be set aside for ceasing, resting, embracing, and feasting. (However, don't forget that this is an ideal—and sometimes our circumstances prevent our being able to practice our vision. Moreover, as we have noted before, we dare not let our Sabbath keeping become legalistic. We are adamant about setting aside the day because we have freely chosen to observe it in response to God's grace, not because we have to fulfill an onerous obligation!)

A few summers ago I was training the camp staff at Okoboji Lutheran Bible Camp in Iowa. That week I had led daily sessions of Scripture study, taught a few extra classes on Lutheran doctrine and ministry to others, taken lots of counseling walks with students on the staff, and given the Sunday-morning sermon. Relaxing over brunch after worship, I heard the announcement that I would be meeting with the junior counselors that afternoon. I gulped—that had not been listed on my planning schedule, and I had made no preparations.

I was faced with a really tough choice. If I had known about the session, I could have prepared for it on Saturday. I don't ever think that it is work for me to teach such a session (or to give a Bible class or sermon on Sunday mornings) as long as I have done the preparation—the work of planning and study—the day before. I enjoy immensely the privilege of teaching and usually feel in the midst of it that I have been ushered into the presence of God—so I'm always grateful for opportunities to speak on Sabbath days.

The struggle over that extra session arose because it was important to me to encourage the junior counselors. I had not devoted any particular time to them during the week, and I did not want them to think that their work was not significant. On the other hand, to prepare a presentation would violate my internal law against working on the Sabbath. The program director said, "Oh, you can just whip something up, can't you?" No— I could, but I did not want to, because even the few little moments that it would have taken to plan something would have been work.

As I prayed about the situation, a new insight struck me. The reason that I was tempted to break my own habit of not working on the Sabbath was that I deeply cared about those high-school kids that served as junior counselors. Perhaps I could love them best by meeting with them and telling them why I did not prepare a talk for them. That way I could even honor the Sabbath more deeply by telling others about the practice of Sabbath keeping.

That afternoon marks a high point in my faith experience. God certainly gave me that insight into how to deal with the situation in a way which was faithful to my desire to keep the Sabbath and yet showed the youth that I cared about them and wanted to support their work. The junior counselors and I met together for quite a long time. I told them why I would not, at the last minute, prepare a talk for them and thereby introduced them to the whole idea of keeping the Sabbath. The session gave me an opportunity to express my affection for them by urging them to enjoy the practice of Sabbath keeping too. The best thing that I can give those I love is an invitation to cease work and worry, to rest deeply in the grace of God, to embrace the values of the Christian community, and to feast physically, emotionally, intellectually, socially, and spiritually.

To decide that you will keep the Sabbath is the most important starting point, and to continue faithfully in that decision even though you are tempted to break it will reap a harvest of blessings. After a grueling year of preparation, I chose not to study the day before my comprehensive exams began because it was the Sabbath, and I received the gift of much greater calm about the exams than I could have otherwise known. Instead of final cramming, I enjoyed immensely a day of worship, of ceasing to worry, of resting with an extra nap, of embracing the goodness of God by reading a fairy tale, of feasting on music and the beauty of the day.

In order to set the day apart, it is important to establish a precise, deliberate beginning and ending. You might want to follow the proper Jewish tradition of beginning and ending at sundown. We dare not legislate for others how to keep the Sabbath, but we must act decisively to establish the point at which this day of ceasing, resting, embracing, and feasting has started and the point at which we have again returned to the workweek.

One of the most important parts of Sabbath keeping is the involvement of the worshiping community. We cannot keep the day alone. Rather, as we invite others to participate with us in honoring the whole day, they can support us in our intentions as well as provide companionship in our activities. Moreover, I have discovered that every time I explain some of my Sabbath practices carefully, it brings a gift to my listeners, because they then contemplate their own habits—or lack of them—for Sabbath keeping.

Tom, a dear friend who was a trusted mentor of mine when I was in college, helped me understand one of the greatest benefits of my own Sabbath-keeping practice. At a time a few years ago when I was very discouraged and turned to Tom for counsel, I told him that I felt very far from God, that I was ashamed of the weakness of my own spirituality, and that in my discouragement I felt that I could not serve God very well in my teaching and writing.

Tom urged me not to be too hard on myself and said that he saw evidence that my relationship with God was intact, even though I did not *feel* that way. When I asked for specifics, he said, "You keep the Sabbath." That very discipline was causing me to abide in Christ, even though I could not feel anything of his presence.

Too often we base our assessment of our own faith on whether or not we feel good about it. This is comparable to judging one's marriage on the basis of how romantic the partners feel about each other—when the sink is leaking, the children are screaming, the bills need to be paid, and the husband or wife has been laid off from the job. The fact is that God is always gracious; we can always count on his love for us, even when we are not tangibly experiencing it. Furthermore, our faith is his gift, to be nourished by our spiritual disciplines—but these, too, are made possible by his grace.

I have used the word *habit* positively in this book. The great benefit of good spiritual habits is that they enable us to practice the presence of God objectively—by reading his Word, spending time in prayer, worshiping, observing the Sabbath—even when positive subjective feelings are not there.

I am so grateful to my parents for instilling in me from earliest childhood the habits of regular worship and tithing. The result is that I never even have to ask myself on a Sunday morning whether I feel like going to worship or at the beginning of a month whether I feel like giving God a certain percentage of my income. Feelings never even enter the picture, and I don't ever have to waste time trying to make a choice. The habits are there—positively, constructively freeing me to live according to these "childhood" values that I have confirmed as mine in my adulthood. I am not advocating unquestioned habits, but, when we have come to embrace certain values, positively developed habits enable us to live according to them more easily and consistently.

The habits of Sabbath keeping include calling to God even in his apparent absence. In obedience, we learn that God is always present, and that one of the places he is especially present is in the day that he himself has hallowed. I don't think I really understood that until now, as I am writing about it. Certainly that is one of the reasons that God ordained the keeping of the Sabbath day, for in that practice we will always know his presence, even in the dark nights of the soul when he seems to be absent.

Writing the preceding paragraphs makes me want all the more fervently to be faithful in keeping the Sabbath. I am about to leave for a theological convention at which sessions are held on Sunday mornings. I had not yet decided whether to attend one of those sessions or to try to find a sanctuary within walking distance where I could worship—but the decision has just been made clear to me. If I am to be faithful to what I know about my own Sabbath-keeping practices, I have to realize that, if I skip worship, the day will flow into the rest of the week and lose its distinctiveness as the holy day.[2]

In the Christian community we need each other in order to grow in our faith and in our practice of the faith. If these comments have been helpful to you in establishing an intentionality for Sabbath keeping or in suggesting practices for keeping the day holy, I am grateful to God for the privilege of writing this book. If you have suggestions or criticisms, I would be very thankful if you would send them to me, because I want my theological errors to be corrected and my own Sabbath practices to be deepened.[3]

Let us grow together as we seek to keep the Sabbath. This book is full of theologizing, of memories, of practices—but nothing can capture the mystery of the Sabbath, the peace of God's eternal presence in that day, except the intentional choice of welcoming it and honoring it. Perhaps we can catch a glimpse of it in this excerpt from Abraham Heschel's description of the evening worship that begins the Jewish Sabbath:

> Before the last stanza [of a hymn about the redemption of Jerusalem] the congregation rises and turns to the west as a sign of welcoming the invisible guest. They all bow their heads in greeting.
>
> *Come in peace, crown of God,*
> *Come with joy and cheerfulness,*

---

2. I must especially stress here that I am not trying to legislate what choices others should make at this convention, nor will I accuse them of a lack of piety if they choose to hear the readings of some papers instead of attending worship. However, I have been grateful for the model of the Jewish professors I know who participate in the convention; they are faithful in attending the synagogue on their Sabbath day.

3. To contact the author, write or call Marva J. Dawn, 304 Fredricksburg Way, Vancouver, WA 98664, ph. (206) 693-5436.

Amidst the faithful, precious people . . .
Come, Beloved, meet the Bride.

The Sabbath comes like a caress, wiping away fear, sorrow and somber memories. It is already night when joy begins, when a beautifying surplus of soul visits our mortal bones and lingers on.

We do not know how to thank and to say:

With wisdom Thou openest the gates of heaven . . .
Thou changest times . . .
Thou rollest away darkness before light . . .
Thou makest the distinction between day and night.

But there is something greater than the marvel of the world: the spirit. In His world we sense His wisdom, in His spirit we see His love.

With eternal love Thou hast loved the house
of Israel.
Torah, mitzvot, laws and judgements Thou hast
taught us.
Mayest Thou never take away Thy love from us.

Then we hear again the words of Moses urging us to learn how to reciprocate the divine love.

Thou shalt love The Lord, Thy God
With all thy heart, with all thy soul,
And with all thy might . . .

Then we read the words of God:

Remember to do all the commands of the Lord, and
ye will not follow the desires of your heart and
your eyes that lead you astray.
I am the Lord your God, who brought you out of
the land of Egypt to be your God; I am the Lord
your God.

And this is the response:

True and certain is all this,
He is the Lord our God, no one else, and we Israel
are His people.

If we only had enough spirit to comprehend His sovereignty, to live in His kingdom. But our mind is weak, divided our spirit.

> *Spread Thou over us Thy shelter of peace,*
> *Direct us aright with Thine good counsel . . .*
> *Save us for Thy name's sake.*[4]

I especially love that last stanza for its New Testament fulfillment. In the person of Jesus Christ, God has spread over us the shelter of peace as the Word tabernacled among us (John 1:14), and in our faith we anticipate the end of time when he will tabernacle among us forever (Rev. 21:3). Meanwhile, God counsels and directs us through the gift of the Holy Spirit. Out of his great love he sent us a Savior and continues daily to save us from all that would take us away from him. All these gifts we celebrate and know more deeply in the festival of the Sabbath. In our honoring of that day we begin to comprehend his sovereignty and to live more ultimately in his kingdom.

When the Sabbath is finally fulfilled, our divisions and weaknesses will *cease* forever. We will *rest* eternally in God's grace and love. We will *embrace* his kingdom and sovereignty ultimately and perfectly. We will *feast* unceasingly in his presence.

---

4. Heschel, *The Sabbath: Its Meaning for Modern Man* (New York: Farrar, Straus & Giroux, 1951), pp. 68-70.

Appendix

A Few Suggestions for Rituals to Begin and End the Sabbath Day*

At the beginning of the Sabbath day (Saturday evening), light two candles (since the Exodus account of the Sabbath commandment says "Remember" and the Deuteronomic says "Observe"). While lighting the candles, say, "Blessed art Thou, O LORD our God, King of the Universe, who hast sanctified us by Thy commandments and commanded us to kindle the Sabbath lights."

Then give a greeting to the angels, such as "Peace to you, ministering angels, messengers of the Most High." (If you have an angel figure, you might place it near the candles.) The greeting can be extended into a prayer to God—thanksgiving for the protection of the angels, petitition that we might serve God as the angels do in Joy and gladness. . . .

Then the Sabbath prayers can continue in whatever manner the Spirit moves. It is especially valuable to pray

---

* Prepared for retreat participants at Okoboji Lutheran Bible Camp, Milford, Iowa

for the Church,
for pastors, congregational musicians, and anyone else who
   will assist,
for the worship service and your participation in it,
for Christians all over the world as they worship, and
for the unity of the global Church.

You might also pray for the activities of your Sabbath day—
that they might be restful and that you might cease from all work,
worry, anxiety, productivity, needing to be God, striving to create
your own future, and so forth. Pray also that your Sabbath might
be a time of embracing people and Christian values, of feasting
and intimacy, laughter and delight.

End the Sabbath welcoming with these words: "Blessed art
Thou, O LORD our God, King of the Universe, that you have commanded us to observe the Sabbath day and keep it holy."

(This ceremony is called the Kiddush, which means a
sanctifying or setting apart of the day. The ceremony marks a
decisive time of setting aside all of our work so that the Sabbath
can be a time of ceasing, resting, embracing, and feasting.)

At the close of the Sabbath day (Sunday evening), begin
with a lighting of the candles and the kindling prayer, as well as
a greeting to the angels. The Havdalah or farewell prayers include thanking God for all the gifts of the special day—the worship, relationships, fun activities, special foods, and other special
things that you have enjoyed during the day. The prayer closes
with an expression of longing for the next Sabbath day to come
and yearning for the day when Christ will come to take us to his
perfect Sabbath rest. This ceremony, like the Sabbath welcoming, ends with the words: "Blessed art Thou, O LORD our God,
King of the Universe, that you have commanded us to observe
the Sabbath day and keep it holy."

These are just suggestions! Anything that you choose to do
to make the Sabbath celebration meaningful for your family is
fine—the goal is to have a special day set apart for praising God
and trusting his grace.

Works Cited

Bacchiocchi, Samuele. *Divine Rest for Human Restlessness: A Theological Study of the Good News of the Sabbath for Today.* Rome: Pontifical Gregorian University Press, 1980.

Baillie, John. *A Diary of Private Prayer.* New York: Charles Scribner's Sons, 1949.

Barrett, Lois. *The Way God Fights: War and Peace in the Old Testament.* Scottdale, Penn.: Herald Press, 1987.

Beechy, Leonard. "Three Levels of Prayer." *Gospel Herald,* 20 Nov. 1984, pp. 805-6.

Berg, Philip S. *Kabbalah for the Layman: A Guide to Cosmic Consciousness, An Opening to the Portals of Jewish Mysticism.* The Old City Jerusalem: Press of the Research Centre of Kabbalah, 1981.

Berkovitz, Eliezer. *Not in Heaven: The Nature and Function of Halakha.* New York: Ktav, 1983.

Boyer, Ernest, Jr. *A Way in the World: Family Life as Spiritual Discipline.* San Francisco: Harper & Row, 1984.

Cazelles, Henri. *Études sur le Code de l'Alliance.* Paris: Letouzey et Ané, 1946.

Childs, Brevard S. *The Book of Exodus: A Critical, Theological Commentary.* Philadelphia: Westminster Press, 1974.

214

Dawn, Marva J. *I'm Lonely, LORD — How Long? The Psalms for Today.* San Francisco: Harper & Row, 1983.

Day, Dorothy. *The Long Loneliness: An Autobiography.* San Francisco: Harper & Row, 1981.

Downey, Michael. *A Blessed Weakness: The Spirit of Jean Vanier and l'Arche.* San Francisco: Harper & Row, 1986.

Edwards, Tilden. *Sabbath Time: Understanding and Practice for Contemporary Christians.* New York: Seabury Press, 1982.

Ellul, Jacques. *The Ethics of Freedom.* Trans. and ed. Geoffrey W. Bromiley. Grand Rapids: William B. Eerdmans, 1976.

————. *The Humiliation of the Word.* Trans. Joyce Main Hanks. Grand Rapids: William B. Eerdmans, 1985.

————. *Money and Power.* Trans. LaVonne Neff. Downers Grove, Ill.: InterVarsity Press, 1984.

————. *The Technological Society.* Trans. John Wilkinson. New York: Vintage Books, 1964.

————. *The Technological System.* Trans. Joachim Neugroschel. New York: Continuum, 1980.

Engel, Diana R. *The Hebrew Concept of Time and the Effect on the Development of the Sabbath.* Washington, D.C.: American University Press, 1976.

Foster, Richard J. *The Celebration of Discipline: Paths to Spiritual Growth.* San Francisco: Harper & Row, 1978.

Grade, Chaim. *My Mother's Sabbath Days: A Memoir.* Trans. Channa Kleinerman Goldstein and Inna Hecker Grade. New York: Alfred A. Knopf, 1986.

Heschel, Abraham Joshua. *The Sabbath: Its Meaning for Modern Man.* New York: Farrar, Straus & Giroux, 1951.

Huggett, Joyce. *Dating, Sex, and Friendship.* Downers Grove, Ill.: InterVarsity Press, 1985.

Hunter, W. Bingham. *The God Who Hears.* Downers Grove, Ill.: InterVarsity Press, 1986.

Jacobson, B. S. *The Sabbath Service: An Exposition and Analysis of Its Structure, Contents, Language, and Ideas.* Trans. Leonard Oschry. Tel Aviv: "Sinai" Publishing, 5741/1981.

Jewett, Paul. *Man as Male and Female: A Study in Sexual Relationships from a Theological Point of View.* Grand Rapids: William B. Eerdmans, 1975.

Luther, Martin. "Treatise on Good Works." Trans. W. A. Lambert.

Rev. James Atkinson. Vol. 44 of *Luther's Works*. Gen. ed. Helmut T. Lehmann. Philadelphia: Fortress Press, 1966, pp. 15-144.

McClain, Carla. "Human 'Clock' Orders Day Off." *Idaho Statesman*.

Mains, David, and Karen Burton Mains. *The God Hunt: A Discovery Book for Men and Women* (Elgin, Ill.: David C. Cook, 1984).

———. "The Sacred Rhythm of Work and Play." *Moody Monthly*, June 1985, pp. 18-21.

Mains, Karen Burton. *Making Sunday Special*. Waco, Tex.: Word Books, 1987.

Miller, Calvin. *The Table of Inwardness*. Downers Grove, Ill.: InterVarsity Press, 1984.

Miller, Hal. "Partnership with Children." *Voices in the Wilderness* 2 (July/Aug. 1987): 6-7.

Millgram, Abraham E. *Sabbath: The Day of Delight*. Philadelphia: Jewish Publication Society of America, 5725/1965.

Neusner, Jacob. *Invitation to the Talmud: A Teaching Book*. Rev. ed. San Francisco: Harper & Row, 1984.

North, Robert. "The Derivation of Sabbath." *Biblica* 36 (1955): 182-201.

Peterson, Eugene H. "Confessions of a Former Sabbath Breaker." *Christianity Today*, 2 Sept. 1988, pp. 25-28.

———. "The Pastor's Sabbath." *Leadership*, Spring 1985, pp. 52-58.

"Sabbaticals Spread from Campus to Business." *U.S. News and World Report*, 25 Jan. 1985, pp. 79-80.

Shenk, Sara Wenger. *Why Not Celebrate!* Intercourse, Penn.: Good Books, 1987.

Sine, Tom. *The Mustard Seed Conspiracy*. Waco, Tex.: Word Books, 1981.

Singer, S. *Sabbath and Holiday Prayer Book*. English trans. New York: Hebrew Publishing, 1926.

Smith, Jeff. *The Frugal Gourmet*. New York: Morrow, 1984.

———. *The Frugal Gourmet Cooks with Wine*. New York: Morrow, 1986.

Stuckey, Charles F., ed. *Monet: A Retrospective*. New York: Park Lane, 1985.

Swartley, Willard M. *Slavery, Sabbath, War, and Women: Case Issues in Biblical Interpretation*. Scottdale, Penn.: Herald Press, 1983.

Talisman, Mark. "The Precious Legacy." New Orleans Museum of Art's *Arts Quarterly* 7 (Jan.-Mar. 1985): 4-9.

"Try Shabbas" (editorial). *Tikkun* 3 (Jan./Feb. 1988): 12-13.

Tsevat, Matitiahu. "The Basic Meaning of the Biblical Sabbath." In *The Meaning of the Book of Job and Other Biblical Studies: Essays on the Literature and Religion of the Hebrew Bible.* New York: Ktav, 1980, pp. 39-52.

Wolin, Sheldon S. *Politics and Vision: Continuity and Innovation in Western Political Thought.* Boston: Little, Brown, 1960.

Wolterstorff, Nicholas. *Until Justice and Peace Embrace.* Grand Rapids: William B. Eerdmans, 1983.

Zborowski, Mark, and Elizabeth Herzog. *Life Is with People: The Culture of the Shtetl.* New York: Schocken Books, 1952.